D1545913

LOVE
AND
CONTROL
IN
SEXUALITY

LOVE
AND
CONTROL
IN
SEXUALITY

NORMAN PITTENGER

A PILGRIM PRESS BOOK
FROM
UNITED CHURCH PRESS
PHILADELPHIA

Library of Congress Cataloging in Publication Data

Pittenger, William Norman, 1905–
    Love and control in sexuality.

    "A Pilgrim Press book."
    "The present book is a slightly expanded version
of the lectures given at West Texas State University
in March 1974."
    1. Sexual ethics. 2. Sex instruction for youth.
I. Title.
HQ31.P67   176   73–19833
ISBN 0-8298-0268-1

United Church Press, 1505 Race Street,
Philadelphia, Pennsylvania 19102

FOR
JAMES AND ANNE BETHELL
WITH AFFECTION
AND GRATITUDE

CONTENTS

PREFACE

Some years ago I wrote a small book called *Making Sexuality Human* (United Church Press, 1970). The book had a very kind reception in many quarters and led to a number of invitations to lecture on human sexuality, most of them from universities or colleges in the United States. These lectures were usually hour-length discussions; but one invitation, to give the Willson Lectures at West Texas State University in Canyon, Texas, was for a series of talks.

The present book is a slightly expanded version of the lectures given at West Texas State University in March 1974. And a few words about their main theme may be useful.

One of the friendly criticisms most frequently heard

about my earlier book had to do with possible "wrong-nesses" in sexual behavior. I had written very positively about human sexuality because I was and am convinced that long years of repression, distaste, sometimes out-right condemnation of sex, not least in circles associated with the Christian churches, are greatly in need of cor-rection by such a positive discussion. My main purpose in *Making Sexuality Human* was to emphasize the essen-tial goodness of sex, and to show that sex is not only central in human experience but is the physiological-psychological basis or ground for man's capacity to love. I realized, of course, that human sexual behavior can be distorted or wrongfully expressed; but I did not say very much about this. My intention was different.

The present book is my attempt to balance the stress in the earlier one. I took the opportunity, afforded me by the invitation to give the Willson Lectures, to take up what I have called "love's controls" of sexual activity. I had used the word controls several times in the first book, but always with a certain hesitation lest I seem to be falling back into a negative or repressive way of talking. However, I was assured—first of all from coun-selling personnel at the Institute of Religion at Texas Medical Center in Houston, where I gave one of my lectures—that this word is a quite respectable one and need not suggest anything negative or repressive. I was told that it could be taken to indicate the right direction of activity implied in any given discipline—that is, such a discipline or procedure requires some "controlling principles" which will enable it to be carried on in the fashion appropriate to the particular enterprise.

I now use the word with an easy conscience, suggesting that in human sexual expression the "controls" are derived from the reality of love as relationship between persons. Whatever works toward true love is good; whatever works against it, in denial or twisting or hurting or otherwise, is not good. Thus, negatively one can say that unsatisfactory or improper sexual behavior is that which is selfish, cruel, impersonal, irresponsible, or "inordinate" (by the last I mean disproportionate to the totality of life in love).

The discussion in this book begins with an introductory chapter on the meaning of specifically *human* sexuality. This is followed by a consideration of the need for "controls" of sexual life, if its overt and genital expression is to be healthy and right. The third section is subdivided into five parts, each dealing with one of the "negatives" mentioned above. Finally, the last chapter returns to an emphasis on the positive goodness of human sexuality.

Some of the material included in this book was also given in lectures at the following places: Texas Christian University, the Institute of Religion at Texas Medical Center, Trinity College in Hartford, Connecticut, Memphis State University, the University of Minnesota, the University of Rochester, and Washington University in St. Louis, Missouri. To the authorities in these places, and above all to those at West Texas State University, I am grateful for the invitations to speak on their campuses and for the kind hospitality shown me while I was with them.

Despite the fact that I talk in this book about "controls," I hope that nobody will read what I have written without coming more firmly to believe that man *is* a sexual being, that this is a *good* thing, that we should never be afraid of sex nor try to run away from it, and that when men and women recognize, accept, and rightly use their sexuality it is both ennobling and splendid and what is more, provides one of our chief clues to how things go in a world whose creative principle is love itself: the God who is cosmic Love or cosmic Lover.

King's College   *Norman Pittenger*
Cambridge, England

THE HUMAN MEANING OF SEXUALITY 1

"Love's controls" of sexual acts and behavior: that is our topic; and at once there is likely to be a protest. Have we not had quite enough of controls? Are we not now enjoying genuine sexual freedom? Does not talk of controls immediately suggest a negative or repressive attitude toward sexual desires and contacts?

Such a probable protest makes it necessary to begin by saying something about the particular sense which we shall be giving to that ambiguous word controls. For there can be no doubt that often enough talk of controls *is* really talk about repression of human instinct and drive. Certainly for a considerable part of Christian history the only kind of control of sexuality which was urged upon men and women or boys and girls was the sort which implies a jaundiced view of sex and has suggested (if not explicitly affirmed) that it would be much better if this awkward aspect of human existence were not so much a lively and inescapable reality. Or if not that, it has been intimated that "before the fall" human sexuality was unaccompanied by strong emotion, physical reactions, and other such "nonrational" qualities. Augustine could speculate on how the first man and the first woman might have been able to procreate in a more "rational" manner, which is to say without the excitement of sex as in our "fallen state" we know and experience it.

Any reader of my earlier book *Making Sexuality Human* should know that the attitude which I commend is vastly different from that. Sex is a good thing, sexual desires and drives are also good, the excitement in sexual contact is good—of all this I am entirely convinced; and it is unnecessary to repeat the arguments which I adduced for this basic goodness. It is important, however, to insist that when we are talking about "controls" in such a context we are talking about something that is very positive, that affirms the goodness of human sexuality, and that is concerned only with seeing to it that the very best expression of human sexuality is made possible for the human race.

In a word, we shall be thinking of *love's* controls; and to put it that way ought to make the point clear. If human sexuality is the ground or base for human loving it is also the expression of human loving; this means that its concrete expression in genital activity and associated behavior must be related to love in the most intimate fashion. Love is the reference, love is the criterion, and love is the basic significance of human sex. And the controls which are to be suggested and discussed have for their sole purpose the securing of precisely that reference, criterion, and significance. The controls are exercised by and in the interests of love; they are not arbitrary, imposed from outside, legalistic, and hence essentially negative, but inherent in love itself and hence essentially positive.

Before we proceed, it may be useful to make some preliminary comments about perspective. It is, or ought to be, a truism that anything said about any topic, save perhaps in the field of exact science as it approximates pure mathematics, will be largely if not wholly determined by the stance which is taken. Provided that the facts of the case are recognized for what they are, we see and interpret and speak about them from a particular point of view. Therefore I must indicate the perspective from which I am writing in this book. Then the reader can make such allowances as his generosity will permit him, in respect to what is actually being said on the subject.

So, I confess that I look at the human meaning of sexuality as a Christian believer—not very happy about much traditional church teaching to be sure, but nonetheless convinced of the essential truth of the Christian vision and glad to profess myself a practicing Christian. I also look at human sexuality as one who recognizes himself to be a sexual being with sexual desires and drives in which I rejoice. And finally, I look at the matter as a believer in a particular conceptuality or philosophical position which has significant religious and moral implications. This conceptuality is called "process thought"; and for our present purpose its most important aspect is its insistence on the dynamic or "becoming" nature of everything in the world, including man himself; and along with this, its insistence on the societal or interrelational quality of everything including man.[1]

To speak of man in "process" terms demands that we speak of him as no static, fixed, unchanging being but rather as a "becoming"—a dynamic movement or direction in which each man is going forward to an actualizing of his potentialities or is failing to go forward to that actualizing. Man is "on the way" to becoming that which is potentially "given" as his possibility; and he is becoming in the community of other men, to whom he is related, by whom he is affected, and upon whom he himself exerts influence.

This is the general perspective, then, which will be adopted in this book: Christian conviction, awareness of the reality and importance of sex, and a "process" way of looking at everything, especially human nature and its development.

This chapter has for its title "the *human* meaning of sexuality"; and I stress the adjective human in order to make clear that like any thoughtful reader I know that while man is not alone in being sexual nevertheless he is sexual in a distinctive way: the *human* way. Despite the obvious truth that humans act like animals in many

---

[1] A fuller discussion may be found in my *Process Thought and Christian Faith* (New York: Macmillan, 1968).

aspects and areas and although they are "equipped" sexually with the same kind of organs as are members of the higher animal kingdom, humans are *not* merely complicated and sophisticated simians nor can their sexuality be reduced to simple animality. Whatever may be the case with creatures in the animal world, man's sexual nature has its specific human characteristics; and these make it different from even though it is related to animal sexuality. What is this distinctively *human* meaning of sexuality?

In *Making Sexuality Human* I sought to work out *how* man's sexual nature is given its specifically human character. I need not repeat what was written there. My present purpose is simply to consider how a *Christian* reading of manhood, using the insight of a "process" conceptuality, looks at the inescapable sexual quality attaching to all human existence. Further, our purpose is to "spell out," as we might style it, the presence in specific human sexuality of such proper modes of expression, of act and behavior, as shall genuinely satisfy and fulfill that humanly understood sexual nature. I have indicated that this implies controls and to speak in that fashion suggests that human sexuality is not at its best when it is entirely unregulated, unrestricted, or indeed nearly promiscuous if not entirely so. The human *expression* of sex, in overt or latent ways, through genital activity and other physical contacts, must somehow be related most intimately to the truly human meaning of sexuality itself.

For a long time a fairly simple answer to the question what is the distinctively human meaning of sexuality, would have run along these lines: human sexuality is for the procreation of children and hence for the continuing propagation of the human race. That answer is still given in many circles, above all in many professedly Christian ones. But it misses out on what is in fact the important point: the *human* meaning of sexuality. It reduces this sexuality to the animal level since procreation is the obvious biological result of most, if not all, sexual contacts. In such an answer there is nothing that is at all distinctively human. It is odd that in certain papal documents, largely intent on stressing the sacred character of human sexual union, this fairly obvious point has been forgotten. In recent years, indeed, due recognition has been given to companionship and love and the way in which sexual union physically speaking can manifest these; but the emphasis seems really to be found elsewhere. Perhaps it is unfair to say this, but the impression is given that in these documents and in similar statements from non-Catholic writers the old fear of sex lingers on, somewhat tempered to be sure, but still a present fact. To move away from the centering of attention on the procreative aspect of genital union seems to imply, for many in these circles, an open invitation to license, promiscuity, or (at best) careless and unconcerned sexual activity, which surely is absurd!

But if we feel obliged to reject this answer to our question, what shall we put in its place? I should suggest that the place to start is by seeing that human sexuality as a physiological and psychological reality is the basis or ground for the human capacity to love and to receive love from another or others. In a word, the deepest meaning of *human* sexuality as distinct from other kinds, is its providing the possibility for a person as a total organic being to exist in a relationship of love with others of his race. This implies, for a Christian at any rate, that sexuality is also a grounding for response to God *in love* and hence a clue to the nature of God himself *as Love*. We shall say something more about this in our last chapter. At the moment it is the human side of the matter to which we must give our attention.

Some may think that it is rather daring to speak of human sexuality as the basis or ground for the human capacity to love. But as Nietzsche once remarked "The degree and kind of a man's sexuality reach up into the ultimate pinnacle of his spirit."[2] The physiological equipment, the total glandular condition, the psychological drives and desires, and the emotional associations of sex are all of them a natural part of man's existence. And since in man as he moves forward in his "becoming," every aspect, physical and spiritual, is interrelated as we know from modern study, it follows inevitably that what goes on in any part of him conditions and affects every other part, spirit included.

Love, intensive and personalized as it is in human beings, or taken in terms of inevitable relationships in a world which (as Teilhard once said) is in process of "amorization," is what holds things together. This does not necessarily mean the kind of passion for others or an other found in human relationships when love is at

[2] Friedrich Nietzsche, *Beyond Good and Evil*, Walter Kaufman, trans. (New York: Random House, 1966), p. 81.

its highest; it includes all the deep contacts in which
sharing, participation, and give-and-take are present and
at work. Of course we see this most vividly at our own
level; but those who like this writer take the "process"
view are convinced that ours is a societal (or in the word
used by Alfred North Whitehead, the father of this
conceptuality, an "organismic") affair, with interpenetra-
tion and interrelationship everywhere. Absolute separation is impossible in fact, even though some may wish
for it in their own experience. Such mutual dependence
and belonging, then, as a characteristic of the entire
creation, comes to its focus in the human reality of love.
That is what we are being made for; that is what we
are "becoming"—if we are *not* moving in that direction
we are going contrary to the grain of the universe, to
how things "go" in the world. The result then is frustration, diminishment of selfhood, and loss of human value.

So just here the process view is of great help to us.
The English writer A. B. Woollard in his book entitled
Progress: A Christian View has observed that "it is in
the controversial field of sexuality that the process
theologians have made their . . . real contribution to
ethical thought today"; and he is kind enough to mention the writer of the present volume as one who has
been influential in this respect. He goes on to say of
sexuality, "This is one area where, because of the profound element of 'mystery' in interpersonal relationships, the secular kind of pragmatism has little to offer."[3]

---

[3] A. B. Woollard, *Progress: A Christian View* (London: S.P.C.K.,
1972), p. 67.

I believe he is correct and that the reality of the "mystery" in sexuality, crowning and focusing "interpersonal relationships," is not sheer dimness nor obscurity but the expression of something which runs through the whole creation: the mysterious yet patent fact of mutual, pervasive, and primarily persuasive give-and-take at every level.

Thus we begin our portrayal of the human meaning of sexuality by affirming sexuality—physiological, psychological, emotional, in a word sensuous—as the inescapable condition for what so often is mistakenly regarded as a purely "spiritual" matter, the wonder of love and its working. Nor is there any reason for religiously minded people to think that this is an unfortunate business. Above all, Christians ought to rejoice in it, since their faith finds its center in the declaration that God himself was "made *flesh*" in the man Jesus and that because that has happened all flesh and all fleshly things are good. They are God's creation and they are the means by which he discloses himself to his children. As I have remarked elsewhere, Christians ought not to attempt to be more spiritual than God himself! If he made and is making us as sexual creatures, and if in Christst -and in other ways elsewhere—he has been and is willing to use flesh and its several aspects to reveal himself, we had better accept the fact.

Writing about this Dom Aelred Graham has pointed out that "the sensuous and the spiritual are not meant to be entirely separated." He notes that while "sensuality alone" can lead to what he calls "incontinent promiscuity, extinguishing all awareness of the spiritual," it is equally true that "the aim of being purely spiritual can terminate in an arid in-humanity, helpful to no one, least of all oneself."[4] This healthy understanding is fortunately increasingly evident in religious and Christian circles and the negative attitude associated with certain varieties of "post-Puritan" religion and morality is much less frequently found.

Thus each man is spirit *and* flesh, or "soul *and* body" as we have been accustomed to say. His spirit or soul is not intruded upon or added to his bodily nature as ancient Greek thought and much traditional "idealism" has assumed. The spirituality of man is integral to him as a whole but so also is his sensuous or fleshly aspect. The two belong together and function together in everything we say and do and are. At the same time, nobody lives to himself alone. As we have said earlier, this tells us that we are deeply *social* beings as well as physical and spiritual ones.

This social nature of persons is almost universally recognized and stressed these days. No longer do we have many thinkers who would talk as if "rugged individualism," each man of and for himself, were the truth. We depend upon one another, we find our best self-expression in contacts with one another, and so we are prepared to agree with the words put into God's mouth by the writer in Genesis: "It is not good for man to be alone." A "helpmeet" (as Genesis puts it), and other people too, are necessary for human life to be

[4] Dom Aelred Graham, *The End of Religion* (New York: Harvest Books, 1971), p. 38.

fully human. Of course this need not require constant physical propinquity; it is not true that "the more we are together" in the sense of concrete physical presence, "the happier we shall be." Sometimes a degree of "solitariness," to use Whitehead's word, is necessary for us; but this does not imply that on those occasions we are utterly separated from our fellows. There is a difference between the fact of our "social belonging" or "togetherness" as a condition of manhood, on the one hand, and always being "in a crowd," on the other.

In this social aspect of our common personhood we can help or hurt others. What we say or do can be *toward* their proper fulfillment in relationship or it can be *away from* that fulfillment. This is where love comes in. Love is relationship of the type that gives as well as receives; it is openness and readiness to help; it is concern, caring, understanding, sympathy, and willing and working for the good of the other or of others. It may be expressed in the present-day demand for justice for all without regard to race, gender, class, creed, nationality, social status or intellectual powers. But it is also to be expressed, and most humanly so, in those more direct "interpersonal relationships" of which Woollard wrote. Then there is an "I-thou" contact—or if not always so intensive as that, an "I-you" one where others are seen as like ourselves in being personalities in the making. In whatever fashion this sociality of man is manifested, its central importance is patent to any thoughtful person today. In social contacts of the less vivid sort as well as in more intimate ones human sexuality is present. Some have the absurd idea that in friendship, for example, there is no sexual component. But this could not be the case since each person is the body-mind complex we have described and everything about them, including their friendships, involves this physiological-psychological base. Freud was getting at this universal quality of sexuality when he wrote about the libido; and others have done the same when they talk of the "erotic nature of human personality." Unfortunately the words "libido" and "erotic" often have a bad connotation for many people; but they should not be so understood. They are simply terms to indicate the basic sexual reality in man. In friendship, of course, there will probably be little, if any, overt sexual activity. We like to be with our friends, to enjoy them, and to share with them so far as possible. In other words we are "in love with them" in a nonintensive way. But thus to be "in love" does not demand that we "have sex" in an explicit or genital fashion. Nevertheless I "love" my friends not with my mind only but also with my body for I "love" them with my whole self or they are not genuinely my friends.

We have spoken about man as a "becoming." He is no fixed entity, no finished product; he is on the way, moving toward fulfillment of possibilities. In this respect he is like everything else in the world. Just as "a pulse of existence" of any sort is in process, so also "what a human being normally accomplishes in the course of his life" is along these lines: "the world gives him his material, his many alternative potentialities, and of these he fashions his personality, which embodies the perspective and the feeling with which he now takes in the world."[5] From the Christian point of view, this is equivalent to saying that out of the created stuff of the world, in all its materiality, there emerges a being who can use this stuff and by his own decisions move in the direction which will most adequately make him a genuine person: a child of God; and because a child of God one who is being created through the divine Love and through his own choices to become a lover. He will be a creaturely, finite and human lover naturally enough; but he is being made and he is making himself *toward that end*. Or, as Christian faith might phrase it, "toward the image of God" which will both reflect and manifest the Love that is originative in God himself.

I trust that it is now evident how a Christian perspective, an acceptance of the fact of human sexuality and a process conceptuality unite to give us an impressive picture of what it means to be human; and hence of the *human* meaning of our sexuality. Like all living creatures we are sexual; but this common fact is given distinctive coloring and qualification in the human case. Thus we can see that to reduce man's sexuality to the level of the barn yard is as bad as to exalt man to the level of the angels. He is neither animal nor angel; he is man, a *human* being.

Despite what must be called their mistake of focusing on the procreative side of human sexual contacts, the papal documents to which we have referred are correct in giving high commendation to marriage. For most

[5] Victor Lowe, *Understanding Whitehead* (Baltimore: Johns Hopkins Press, 1962), p. 20.

members of the human race the "estate of matrimony," entered upon "reverently, discreetly, advisedly, soberly, and in the fear of God" (as the Prayer Book marriage service puts it), is the usual way of finding sexual union and hence the expression of human sexuality. The old English marriage service says that this estate does not exist nor should it be used "to satisfy men's carnal lusts and appetites, like brute beasts that have no understanding." The language is infelicitous but the point is valid; it is but another way of saying what has been said earlier in this chapter: that *human* sexuality is distinctive of man and is not merely that of the animal world. As human beings a man and a woman can come together in this married state and find "mutual society, help, and comfort . . . both in prosperity and adversity." Thus the sexuality which is the natural basis or ground of their human love is given full recognition; at the same time it is set in the context of a wider and more inclusive relationship—a relationship, to continue from the Prayer Book, which is "for better for worse, for richer for poorer, in sickness and in health," and in which both parties, husband and wife, undertake to "love and to cherish" one another "till death them do part."

This is the pattern for the majority of members of the race and although it may not always be maintained— for there can be the "irretrievable collapse" of a marriage, as for example the law in Britain now explicitly affirms—it does as a matter of observable fact serve its purpose admirably for most people. It is an abiding expression of the human meaning of sexuality and is to be seen as "honorable among all men," given full respect, and protected so far as may be from rupture or damage. Here we have the explanation of the persistence of marriage, in one form or another, in all cultures; and in our Western society (elsewhere too, of course) its persistence in a monogamous form—man and wife united to establish a new cell of human society. In this cell, as a result of sexual union, children will very likely be born. They will be cared for and loved, given a home, surrounded by parental help as in their turn they grow to maturity and at length go out into the world, in most instances doubtless to repeat the process for themselves.

Heterosexual union in marriage, genital expression of that union as the couple may decide, establishment of a family with children; this is so much the usual pattern that we take it for granted as being "normal" for persons. It would be better to think of it as *usual*, especially for us today to think in this way, since we now know that for a percentage of the race—some say just short of ten percent, in fact—the sexual attraction is to somebody of the same sex and not to somebody of the other sex. In any modern discussion of sexuality in the human sense it is of the first importance to recognize the presence among us of many homosexually inclined men and women. The time is past when they could be neglected, not to say rejected.

I make my own the words of a letter writer in a recent issue of the Cambridge (England) daily newspaper: "They are not disgusting nor pitiful. A homosexual is a person with a propensity toward his own sex, not a criminal or one with a disease. They are people who in an intolerant society have been subject to mockery and vindictiveness." In a word, the homosexual members of our society are not deviant, but different from the majority; and like all minorities they have their rights as well as their responsibilities. Enough has been written recently to make it unnecessary to continue here this discussion of the "case" for the homosexual—see, for example, the symposia *The Same Sex* (Philadelphia: United Church Press, 1967) and *Is Gay Good?* (Philadelphia: Westminster Press, 1971); and my *Time for Consent* (London: S.C.M. Press, revised edition 1970) as well as the briefer discussion in *Making Sexuality Human*.

In the homosexual's case marriage as such cannot take place but there can be (and often is) a manner of living together which, while different from marriage, is no less "honorable," no less to be respected, no less to be protected (so far as may be) from rupture or damage. Granted that this union is difficult for many homosexuals to achieve, not least because of social attitudes, nevertheless anyone who knows homosexual men and women knows too that they urgently desire some such union with as much permanence as can be managed. They recognize perfectly well that brief encounters, furtive contacts, and "cruising," with "one-night stands" as the result, do not really satisfy. One of them said, "I want to make love and not just have sex." And that remark is equally applicable to persons of heterosexual inclination, for "to make love" is to give the specifically genital contact its finest and most enriching context;

while "having sex" may very well be, and is, highly pleasant in performance but taken alone is an unsatisfactory substitute for the *real* desire of human beings sexually speaking. For the most part—one might almost venture to say, universally—human beings want, sometimes want desperately, a shared life in love, in which physical acts are the expression of that love and not *merely* sensual gratification. This is how *wholeness* is both expressed and attained. As Dr. Jack Dominian has recently written, "The primary purpose of sexuality in each and every sexual act is first of all to secure the relationship of love of the couple."[6]

At the same time, however, *all* sexual behavior or conduct requires a measure of *control* if it is to be realized at its best. Indeed every good thing known to us is in need of some such controlling. "The best may become the worst," says the old adage. This is as true in sexual matters as anywhere else. That is why our next chapter will look more fully at this business of controls, while the central section of this book will speak in detail about such controls and how they are necessary in practice.

[6] Jack Dominian, *The Tablet*, Dec. 2, 1972, p. 1141.

CONTROLS FOR SEXUAL BEHAVIOR 2

The folk wisdom which has been handed down through the centuries has always known that there are ways in which human sexuality may be most satisfactorily and properly expressed and ways which are less satisfactory and in one sense or another harmful to men. The "rules," as we may call them, have varied from place to place and from age to age, but "rules" of some sort there have always been—even when they have not been much followed.

Furthermore, the common man and his spokesman the prophet or seer or moralist, has always been disturbed when no "rules" are followed and when sheer libertinism in sexual activity is prevalent in the circles which he knows. Sometimes this attitude merely represents narrowmindedness and perhaps an envy of others because they do what *we* should like to do if we dared. On the other hand it would be silly to think that a Paul, among Christians, or a Juvenal, among pagan Romans, was like that. Each of them in his own way and out of his own moral presuppositions felt a sense of dismay and horror at sexual libertinism in the Roman Empire. Paul states his opinion in no uncertain terms in such passages as the latter part of the first chapter of his letter to the Romans (where unfortunately he lets his Jewish prejudice make homosexual acts the most offensive of all sexual behavior—but this can be understood, if not accepted, in view of his background). Juvenal in his *Satires*, which many of us must have read in university if we did any study of the ancient classics, is much more outspoken and even vituperative. And so it has been throughout history. We may, perhaps must, reject the totally negative view taken by many of the spokesmen for the common man. But we must certainly recognize that sexual behavior in an entirely unrestricted fashion is hardly conducive to the best interests of men and women if they are genuinely to become lovers and not simply gratify impulse whenever they have the urge to do so.

I have always felt that some such principles of sexual behavior were necessary for people if they were to act *humanly* and not descend to the level of "the beasts that perish"—and even lower than that since after all the beasts act according to their natural pattern and can hardly be described as "lustful" in a pejorative sense. But it would never have occurred to me to use the word controls here had I not had many conversations with workers in scientific fields, particularly psychologists, sociologists, and those concerned with "social care." From them I have learned that the word controls (which to me had had an unpleasant sound) is a perfectly good and frequently employed term for the conditions under which research and enquiry may be carried out in the best fashion possible with most assurance of sound results and in accordance with the requirements of the particular subject matter under investigation. After I had expounded to these acquaintances and friends my notion that there were implicit principles which governed rightful and healthy sexual behavior, they told me that I should speak of these principles as "controls." I do not wish to put on my associates the blame for my use of the term; but their hearty commendation of its use gives me the courage to employ it and also the right to ask my readers to understand it in the positive sense which those associates gave to it in our conversations.

I learned something else from these talks; and that is the point that in any enquiry requiring controls there must be some major reference in terms of which the controls are to be applied. This gave me a challenge to think; I came to the conclusion that because of love's having its basis or ground in the physiological-psycho-logical-emotional-spiritual reality of sexuality, the proper reference must be *love itself*. In this chapter, then, I am speaking about *love's* controls exercised over and upon sexual behavior as a way of securing the best, most satisfactory, and most fulfilling expression of all that goes to make up our human sexual nature.

That the best may be corrupted into the worst is a bit of human wisdom that we must never forget. It is just here that the need for controls comes so forcibly into the picture. A man of great genius can become a man with enormous capacity for doing evil. Somebody with remarkable personal appeal (a Hitler is an instance) can exercise that appeal in a way that is disastrous for a whole generation. Anybody with good qualities can allow these to be distorted so that they work for evil ends. We all know this quite well both from history and from personal experience. Controls are necessary for us all.

Time and again we have spoken of "becoming" as the characteristic of everything in the world. In the "process" view which I accept this is the central notion; the universe at any and every moment consists of nothing but "becomings" at various levels and in various ways. This applies to man in particular; "he never is, but wholly hopes to be," as Browning once said. Man hopes in that he both yearns for and moves toward what he is not as yet. In him the material which he receives from the past, including at every moment his *own* past, is given its peculiar and special form by whatever is his "defining characteristic" (here I am using Whitehead's precise terminology). For us the defining characteristic is our growth toward becoming genuine lovers in a relationship of caring, concern, self-giving and receiving from others. Toward this as our "subjective aim" (once again, Whitehead's term), we are moving; if not, we are denying our possible manhood and becoming other or less than fully and truly human. There is no abiding *substance* or *thing* called manhood; rather, manhood is a process of becoming men—in biblical language, our "vocation" is to become what in God's purpose or intention we are meant to be.

Now in this movement of people as "a society of occasions"—our past experiences held together by our defining characteristic—decisions must be made by each of us. We are free to make them, for better or for worse. Neither God nor anything else *forces* us to make *this* rather than *that* decision, at least within the limits of our possibility, although, of course, somebody living in the United States in 1974 has different limiting possibilities than somebody living in France in 1620. *Ultimately* the range of possibilities is given its limitations by God. An atheist would disagree here, but we who are both Christians *and* process thinkers are sure that in this respect God is necessary if there is to be any chance of novelty without chaos—the past alone could not provide the requisite lures or opportunities, nor can a thinker who accepts meaning in the cosmos assume that such things "just happen." Yet within limits we *are* free to decide. Hence the need for self-imposed controls which shall tend to make our decisions the right ones in a proper directional movement forward toward our fullest possible selfhood as lovers.

But freedom carries responsibility with it. We are able to choose, but we know the "ought" in life—the imperative which tells us that we must choose responsibly with regard for the consequences or results of our choosing, not only as these affect *us* in our human becoming, but also as they affect *the others* with whom we have to do. In an interrelated universe like ours and with that same interrelationship at the human level, including on this level both consciously known and unconsciously felt influences from what has gone on around us, such consequences or results are inevitable. For these consequences, following upon the free decisions that each of us has made, any morally sensitive person recognizes his due responsibility. Of course we are not "to blame" for all that follows upon our chosen acts. Circumstances may be such that *this*, rather than *that*, has taken place—we did not will it, desire it, expect it. In the language of an older moral theory we were at this point "invincibly ignorant," since had we been able to know that *this* would take place we should have decided otherwise. But decide we did and so it is that indirectly we must assume some degree of responsibility. When it comes to matters where we *did* know the probable results for ourselves and for others and for good or for ill, the degree of our responsibility is obviously much enhanced.

It may be that some will reject altogether any idea of their having to grow in moral sensitivity, but that is tantamount to saying that such a person refuses to accept one of the factors which make him human. To be human *is* to grow; failure to do so marks us as receding from, or moving out of the way of genuine human advance. To see this does not imply that one must become a moral rigorist; after all, as Whitehead once remarked, "Love is a little oblivious as to morals." On the other hand there is a moral pattern more profound and penetrating than the "moralism" which on the whole is an unpleasant affair.

This moral pattern is simply a line of growth in correspondence with our intentional manhood—as a lover, "in-the-making" of course, yet called to that vocation by virtue of being human. Hence a "proper man"—one who understands what he is to become—cannot fail to sense the responsibility which is his to grow in this fashion and to do whatever is in his power to assist others in their similar growth.

At this point, in order to refute the notion that such a sense of responsibility and an advocacy of controls for sexual behavior implies (despite all that I have said hitherto) a wish to impose my own or even the specifically Christian view on others, it seems necessary to say something in favor of what nowadays is called "the permissive society." It would be tragic if the reader were led to think that a concern for responsibility and its attendant controls means opposition to that type of society and a condemnation of it as a manifestation of decadence.

To my mind a permissive society is a good and not a bad thing. This is not to commend or condone everything that may take place in it. Like any other social pattern, permissiveness can express itself in unpleasant, anti-social and damaging ways. But it *is* to say that a society whose members are given as much freedom as possible to choose for themselves this or that course, is a better society than one in which moral decisions are dictated either by legal code or by conventional practice supposed to be followed without question.

Some of those who are alarmed at the less happy, perhaps even perverse manifestations of permissiveness, have not understood the basic moral issue which ought to be faced. They have failed to see that where there is no chance for free decision within the limits set for persons, there can be no genuine morality at all. In Kapek's play *R.U.R.* men are made into mechanical dolls; they do what they are supposed to do because they are *compelled* to do it. They are not moral beings. But man *is* a moral being—or on the way to becoming one. That is to say, he has a certain genuine if limited freedom and he can assume responsibility for what he chooses in that freedom. This is a central element in his moral character. If he were neither free nor responsible, he would not be a moral being in any significant sense.

Now a permissive society grants, within fairly broad limits and under the requirement that harm shall not be done to others, a freedom to choose. With that freedom, responsibility is required; as we have insisted, the two always go together. If I decide for this or that course of action in respect to my conduct in sexual matters and in all others, I am effectively *using* my freedom. I may be mistaken in my choice; I may be in need of more information, deeper insight, better understanding of the situation and of its probable consequences. Certainly I shall always need some degree of moral courage if I am to take *any* stand; and I find that my best moral instincts require a strengthening which in religious terms is called "grace." But I am free; and I know myself as free.

Naturally there are limits even in such a society. I am not allowed to make a decision of the sort which has for its consequences that I shall murder another, steal from him, or willfully hurt him—this is where controls come in, and in this very general instance they are controls integral to, and with their reference in the possibility of the common life where we can live together without terror and with some assurance that everyone is seeking a common good. Limits are set in *any* society and for that reason. They are based upon the requirement of wider social welfare and of human cooperation. At the same time, when I do choose I am in the position of having to take upon myself a responsibility not only for my decision itself but also for its consequences. To be permitted freedom to decide is to accept responsibility for decisions made.

We hear a great deal these days about the way in which some people choose to buy and read pornographic literature, or attend what are styled "dirty" plays, or engage in what many of their contemporaries would regard as immoral sexual activity. Doubtless many do just these things. But if they are not allowed the freedom to make what others regard as *wrong* choices, the only alternative is control (not in the sense in which we have been using the word, but in a coercive sense) exercised upon them by some human agency, whether it is the state or pressure exerted by social groups or campaigns, or inherited opinion from the past with its prejudices as well as its value, or some similar agency. What guarantee have we that any of these "know best" what men and women should choose? None of them is divine; none of them speaks nor can speak, with absolute authority.

As a Christian I believe that God has left men free to make their decisions within the limits set by their situation and circumstances, and given the range of possibilities open to them. He has not dictated to us what we shall do. Even if our ancestors believed that the Ten Commandments, say, were handed down by God from Mount Sinai, many of us today would probably accept that these commandments (and other such supposed dictates) are a brief statement of Jewish tribal mores with parallels in other areas of the Middle East or Near East. If they are still valid for us, they are valid because they commend themselves to our moral sensitivity and not because they are supposed to be the divine *ipse dixit*. And the so-called "natural law," to which others make their appeal, especially in Catholic circles, is not primarily a set of detailed divinely derived prescriptions implanted in the human heart. As Thomas Aquinas himself said, the "natural law" is the inborn sense that we "should do good and avoid evil"; and its precise directives as generally understood, have been worked out by men for themselves, usually reflecting what was assumed to be "right" in the particular culture in which they found themselves.

Finally, a Christian knows or should know that God is Love and that his purpose for men which they are to make actual in their concrete experience through their own decisions, is that they are to live together in love. Just *how* they are to do that, they must learn for themselves by trial and error, by using their heads, by keeping their eyes open, by listening to the wisdom of their ancestors *and* by recognizing that "new occasions teach new duties." This is *not* antinomianism nor is it complete absence of moral standards or requirements. On the contrary, it is putting the emphasis on the way God wills

men to discover what are such standards and requirements for us where we now are and how we now are.
Again, this is the point at which the controls, integral to
and with their reference in love as the sole absolute, will
come into the picture. But we have seen that controls in
this sense are different from control in the other and
coercive sense.

No Christian, indeed no sensitive humanist, approves
everything that goes on in a permissive society. But he
ought also to know that the alternative to that kind of
society is much worse. And in my judgment he ought to
welcome permissiveness as one fumbling and imperfect
step in the movement toward a state of affairs where
freedom is assumed and responsibility accepted. Doubtless such a state of affairs will not come in fullness, short
of the kingdom of God. Yet we may be grateful for any
approaches to it.

So far we have not considered the question of human
sin. And it may well be asked, how does the religious
concept of sin fit into the picture which has been drawn
in the discussion?

First of all, I am far from suggesting that sin is not
real and hateful. The word sin is often misunderstood
but the reality to which it points is inescapable. One of
the interesting developments in the past thirty or forty
years, and not only in religious and theological circles,
has been the rediscovery of human sinfulness. In the
halcyon days of "liberalism" (in its pre-World War II
sense) many thought that with a little more information,
wider opportunities for education and better organiza-
tion of society, man was likely to become pretty much a

perfect creature. When we had managed to eradicate "the ape and the tiger" in us and in our fellows—that in itself a rather formidable task, one might observe!—all would be well. Bishop Mandell Creighton, the English historian, commented upon this, "The jackass will still remain!" But it is not so much the silliness and stupidity of a man that needs to be got rid of; but, it is his seemingly inveterate readiness to decide for what seems agreeable to his less-developed, less fully human movement toward becoming himself as a participant in the "creative advance" toward shared goodness or love. In other words, there is a *false* "self-centeredness" which is damaging to proper growth for one's own self and for others. And the long-accumulated store of such non-shareable decisions with their consequences, has made decisions *for* love very difficult indeed—sometimes wellnigh utterly impossible. This is the sort of situation and the sort of reality to which the word sin is pointing; it is a terrible situation and a ghastly reality. For once again the possibility of the highest or best can become the occasion for the worst.

This book is not the place for a treatment of the specifically Christian way of seeing the matter and the Christian conviction about what is being done about it by God himself. Suffice it to say that here we have to do with the whole issue summed up in theological textbooks under the title, "Sin and Redemption." Our point now is that responsible contemporary Christian thought does not regard sin as breaking a set of divine commandments the disobedience to which is to be punished by damnation. Rather, it sees sin as essentially the breaking of

right relationships—between man and man and between
God and man. *That* way of putting the matter makes
sin more terrible, more ghastly, than did the older view.
Why? Because to break such relationships given in and
intended for growth in love, is to violate the integrity
of the universe under God who himself is unfailingly
related to it. Thus once more we are back to our insistence that controls are necessary if sin in this profound
sense is not to proliferate.

In the matter of explicit sexual activity, then, whatever we do should be for *good* and for *all*. If it is selfish,
cruel or hurtful, irresponsible, unrelational, inordinate
or without pattern and limits, it will be wrong since it
damages relationships both with others and with God
who is present in what happens in the world. If it is
trustful, aware of others, and hence mutually "bene-
ficial," caring for them and helpful to them, it is right—
it helps us and them to grow toward full manhood in all
its necessary relationships in and under God. It is as
simple and as exacting as that.

But the supreme reference in the controls about
which we are speaking is love itself—love understood as
sharing, mutuality, giving-and-receiving fellowship, as I
have so often insisted; not as sentimentality or laxity
or easy tolerance. The controls are not imposed from
outside nor from on high upon men and women whose
nature bears no relationship to what is being asked of
them. Such a view would be un-human, even anti-hu-
man; and the best Christian insight down the ages has
never succumbed to such a man-denying and man-
negating position, even if *some* who think they repre-

sent that insight have talked that way now and again. Authentic Christianity at this point is authentic humanism; it differs from secularistic humanism in that it has a higher and a deeper grasp of what it means to be human, setting humanity in the context of a divine movement in good and not contenting itself with the proximate or ready-to-hand picture of manhood so often found in secularistic humanism.

The controls are not imposed from on high but are intimately present in human nature itself, since *love* is what man is becoming and is therefore integral to him in that becoming.

In the next part of this book, in five subchapters, we shall look at the ways in which controls may be seen as necessary, indeed as *given*, in the central stress on man's becoming a creaturely or finite lover. I end this chapter with an apology for what perhaps may have seemed to some readers a rather arid and abstract discussion of the background for this consideration of controls. If the discussion has seemed abstract, the thing which has been under discussion is concrete enough. It is something we all know about, experience and feel, although very likely my way of talking about it is not everybody's. Once more, then, I appeal to the opening comment in the first chapter. I have been writing as a Christian, as one who knows himself to be a sexual being, and as a proponent of "process" thought. And I believe, rightly or wrongly, that this has given us a stance or perspective which fits in with and makes sense of common human experience in all its simplicity and in all its strange complexity.

DISTORTIONS IN SEXUAL ACTIVITY 3

In this long chapter we shall look at what I venture to style "distortions of sexual activity"—modes or ways of sexual conduct which militate against the richest and most fulfilling possibilities of sex. It is over such that the controls of which we have spoken are to be exercised; and as it will be recalled this exercise is for the positive purpose of letting love, based as it must be on man's sexual nature, have the opportunity to be itself, its true self, in those moments when a man or woman is intent upon overt sexual behavior.

Having said this, however, I must add that it is in no way my intention to be "judgmental" at this point. It ill befits any of us to judge his fellows; only God is competent to do that, and *his* judgments (unlike most of ours) are tempered by loving-kindness and mercy. No one of us knows enough about the interior life of another person, his motivations, his deepest intentions, his terrible needs, his desire for answers to those needs, his loneliness, his despair, his fears and alarms, as well as his joys, his capacity for self-giving and receiving, his yearning for companionship, to sit in judgment upon him.

What we *can* do, on the other hand, is say that so far as we can see or understand, *this* or *that* particular way of acting is not conducive to the best growth or development in the direction of true manhood. Every particular act done by anybody, is always to be seen in the context of that movement—or as I like to say, the best "directionality" of human existence, or something less than the best "directionality." The particular act is nothing like so important as the way the man or woman *is going;* and one of the worst aspects of human judgment is so to focus on the particular occasion that we fail to see the more comprehensive way forward or backward. Those upon whom has been laid the almost intolerable burden of counselling others or of "hearing their confessions" (either formally or in a manner that is simply friendly and pastoral) need above all to be careful at this point. Out of a considerable experience in this field I am prepared to say that the *most* difficult thing for the counsellor or "confessor" is to put himself alongside another human life and then seek to *feel* its very heartbeat; or, to change the image to the one used a moment ago, to sense the direction of that life and speak helpfully about it to the person who comes wanting

counsel, advice or the assurance of the divine forgive-
ness.

So let us be quite clear that the distortions about
which we are to speak are those whose importance and
whose danger will be found in their long-range occur-
rence, rather than in this or that single incident. But at
the same time, we need to recognize that not infrequently
the single incident can be revealing of precisely that
long-range attitude or manner of behavior. If I tell a lie
on one occasion, this may very well show that I am "becoming a liar"; and *there* is the dangerous side. Ralph
Waldo Emerson once said, "What you are speaks so
loudly that I cannot hear what you say." Perhaps we
could adapt this saying and phrase it as follows, "What
seems to be the indication of a persistent tendency in
your life is so clearly shown in this or that particular
moment, that I cannot help feeling you need to look
more deeply into your motivations and seek the 'purity
of heart' or 'emotional sincerity' to act differently."

In any event, when we grasp the point that every man
is a fascinating and special complex in which the materials he inherits from his own past self, from others and
from the world, are used by his own decision, for or
against his movement toward realizing his vocation as a
man—his "initial aim" in "process" language—we come
to the recognition that each one of us is taking some path
into the future which is either for or contrary to his
most adequate human fulfillment. In a way then, morality
is a matter of degree rather than of sharp and absolute
distinctions.

Sometimes, indeed, people foolishly speak of moral

"black and white," assuming that everything is very clear, very precise, with no shadings of gray or "near-white" and "near-black." Yet a little observation and much personal introspection ought to show us that most of the time we are dealing with just such nuances or shades. This is why I repeat that my own concern here is neither to make judgments nor to speak of what is supposedly *absolutely* wrong in the manifestations of selfishness, cruelty, impersonality, irresponsibility and disproportion seen in men and women in their sexual behavior.

My old acquaintance the late Harry Emerson Fosdick was in his day America's outstanding preacher. His sermons were often summarized in the press on Monday morning. On one occasion he had been preaching at a women's college and had said that human living and loving were always to be such that they might be called "beautiful." The uproar which followed the summary of that sermon in the Monday papers still resounds in my mind. "What has happened to morality? Where are ethical standards? Are young girls at college to be invited to illicit sexual conduct, since they might think it 'beautiful'?" And so the attacks continued, most of them ill-informed and stupid—and most of them, including some sermons preached the following Sunday and then reported in the papers for the day after, from clergymen who ought to have had more sense.

After all I thought then and I think now, is not a "beautiful life" one which is harmonious, well-proportioned, balanced? Is not beauty itself a value of the highest ultimacy? And for a Whiteheadian "process"

Christian anyway, is not the truly *aesthetic*—the deeply-felt and experienced delight in which the whole self is finding its satisfaction or fulfillment in making actual its true potentialities—the very best of all possible moments? To live beautifully *is* to live well, it is to live "the good life"; and Socrates' little prayer, reported by Plato, is to the point: "O Pan, and all other gods who dwell in this place," he said, "make me *kalagathos*," which my Greek lectionary tells me means "good and beautiful, or harmonious."

The trouble with distortions of human sexuality is that they make sexual contacts not beautiful but ugly, not harmonious but discordant. They break into and break up the splendor of human relationships because they are damaging to love. As we turn now to look at some of those distortions we remember that the avoidance of them is through the controls of love, not imposed from outside or from on high but integral to the very nature of love itself. In doing this, in thus controlling human sexual activity, they are furthering the truest interests of men and women for whom growth in love is the intended destiny. How more positive can you be?

In our discussion both heterosexual and homosexual types of contact are to be considered together. This is inevitable once we have taken the general attitude on homosexuality briefly stated in the opening chapter: that the homosexuals among us are not deviant but only different from the majority in their experiencing an attraction to their own sex and not to the other sex. Although a great many people do not seem to appreciate it, homosexual love is obviously present in all human society.

What is more, such love can be as tender, demanding, all-embracing and good for the parties concerned as is heterosexual love. Further, the physical endearments and contacts of homosexuals can also be deep in meaning, both expressing that love and impressing upon the lovers the relationship of self-giving and receiving which is theirs. It is not only ridiculous, it is also shockingly unjust to think that such homosexual acts are by necessity nasty or perverted; it is simple error to think, as some apparently do, that *all* "gay" people are merely out "for what they can get," physically speaking. Some of them are, of course; and so also are some heterosexuals. Most of them urgently desire love; most of them have learned, maybe from bitter experience, that there are no substitutes for that love, least of all the superficially effectual substitute of entirely unloving physical sex.

Thus when we are speaking of "distortions" and the need for controls, we need to remember that there can be "distortion" both in heterosexual behavior and in homosexual behavior; that to engage in homosexual acts is not of itself any more "distorted" than to engage in heterosexual ones; and that controls must apply to both sorts of people. Indeed sometimes when one considers the outrageous domination exercised on occasion by a man over a woman, or a woman over a man, one may be brought to the point of saying that a great deal of homosexual conduct is *less* selfish, cruel, irresponsible, impersonal, and disordered. But we have already said enough to make the position clear. We must now proceed with our discussion.

SELFISH SEXUAL EXPRESSION

Selfish expression of sex is the attempt by one person to procure satisfaction, gratification or pleasure in sexual relationship at the expense of and without due consideration for the other in the contact. That is as simple and direct a definition as can be given. And from that way of defining it the distortion is obvious. Love is not made the point of reference, love does not provide the criterion, and love exercises no control over the acts of the selfish person. But we need to recognize that there is a certain subtlety here, more particularly in respect to the meaning of the word selfish.

In one sense everything that is wrong about human life and experience, both personally and socially, can be summed up in that one word selfishness. Something of the sort is acknowledged by almost all religious and moral teaching, Christian or otherwise. Indeed, some of the greatest contemporary theologians (including William Temple) have often spoken as if we could identify sin with selfishness—and leave it there. Temple himself was a little more cautious, since he discriminated between a false variety of selfishness, which he felt to be the root of sin, and the variety of self-centeredness which is necessary if human existence is to continue. And just at this point it is essential to follow William Temple rather than some of his less careful disciples.

Without some real concern for the self, nobody could live. Without some genuine self-awareness, nobody could live humanly. The trouble comes when this natural and necessary self-concern and self-awareness is carried to the point of carelessness about others, total centering of interest in the self, and the implicit assumption that each of us, man or woman, is "the hub of the universe," "the monarch of all we survey." Everything else and everybody else must revolve around us or be obedient to our wishes and desires. Of course this is unrealistic nonsense, as any thoughtful person knows very well; yet despite its absurdity and lack of realism, it is a very present danger and most of us, much of the time, can succumb to it.

But we do enormous harm when we talk to others in a too glib fashion about their self-concern, failing to make this important distinction. We may *mean* what I should call "false self-centeredness," but we may *say* "selfishness" without any qualification—and then trouble can result.

I think of a boy whom I knew, who in his Sunday school had been taught that all self-concern was wrong. He accepted the statement because he respected his teacher. In consequence he was plunged into utter despair. At his age, moving from childhood through the storm and strife of adolescence with its physiological concomitants and with the inevitable development of emotional life, he was entirely unable to avoid self-concern. He was increasingly aware of himself, his desires, his inner struggles, his insecurity; and the more he tried to kill in himself the self-concern which his teacher had told him was sin, the more confused and disturbed he became. In his case, too, there was the complication of sexual discovery, leading to the practice of masturbation—a quite normal aspect of the typical adolescent as he grows toward maturity. He felt himself to be "the worst sort of sinner," as he put it, not only because of his thinking that self-stimulation sexually was wrong but chiefly because he had been told that the self-awareness which was associated with this practice was the very root of all sin.

Fortunately a wise counselor was able to assist him. But it took considerable effort to get the boy to understand that what he had been told in his Sunday school was a mistaken way of saying something that *is* true: namely, that concern for self *can* be wrong when it becomes so central that one thinks oneself the only important person in the world and seeks only one's own satisfactions without regard or respect for others. It was the falsity of self-concern, in that extreme manifestation, which made it wrong, he now recognized; there was nothing wicked in his natural physiological and psychological condition which led him to be keenly aware of himself as a person who was growing up to be a responsible adult.

But on the other hand there was a woman of about thirty, married for several years, who was in great distress because relations between her husband and herself seemed to be deteriorating very badly. She told the clergyman to whom she came for assistance, that her husband found as many opportunities as possible to remain away from home in the evenings. She said that he even wanted to take his holidays alone and seemed to regard her as something of a nuisance. She said that her husband was "unspeakably selfish," that he was "running away from her," and that he was "doing goodness knows what."

An hour or so was sufficient to reveal the real problem. One did not need to see or talk with the husband to get the point—although later conversation with him was useful in suggesting ways in which he could help his wife. The *real* problem was not her husband's supposed selfishness but her own. She had twisted love in such a way that she regarded the man she had married as if he were simply "hers"; she talked about him as if he were her own possession whom she could dominate and control. And when he responded by asserting his own personal independence as a human being, she was ready to accuse him of being "utterly selfish"—how easy it is to project on others one's own deepest difficulty! In talking with her it was possible to see how this woman was "cannibalistic" in her own subtle way; that is, she wanted and tried to devour her husband. He could have no independence; everything he said or did was judged in terms of her own approval; if she disliked his words or his actions, then he was thought to be "against her," neglecting her, failing to give her all of himself.

Nor was it surprising that the specifically sexual aspect of their married life was going to pieces. She blamed this on him, saying that he failed to cooperate with her. The fact was that while she was not a nymphomaniac, she was a highly sexed woman who wanted and demanded from her husband, continual sexual relations and of a type that (as it happened) were not too pleasing to him. Here, then, was a person who was *falsely* self-centered, acting as if her own gratification (in sexual contacts and in everything else) was all that mattered.

Happily, she was also a person of good sense and

intelligence and basically open to the possibility of reaching a new understanding of the situation. With the help of her husband, who deeply loved her, and with continuing assistance from the clergyman to whom she turned, she learned, first theoretically and then practically, the need for and the ways of sharing or of mutuality with the man she had married—and whom she too loved deeply if mistakenly. Problems remained, to be sure; it took a long time for the two to work out a modus vivendi, despite her new insight. But in due course all turned out for the best. Real love, not a possessive similitude of love, won the day.

Perhaps the problem is caused more frequently by the husband than by the wife in cases of this sort. And nowhere is this so plain as in the way in which a very good and loving man can forget his wife's needs when it comes to their genital relationship. A man can secure his satisfaction and release fairly quickly and easily, while a woman may require more time, more patience, more continuing attention and endearments from her husband before she can achieve genuine sexual satisfaction. Anyone who has counselled married couples knows many instances in which the trouble has centered in quick sexual gratification by the husband, who thereupon turns over and goes to sleep, leaving his wife frustrated and uneasy. This lack of concern on the husband's part is a classical instance of what is meant by selfishness in sexual behavior, producing and also reflecting a much deeper distortion in the understanding of love's own demands and requirements.

In each of the instances just cited, selfishness is part

of the picture. In the case of the young adolescent the selfishness was really nothing more than natural and proper self-concern; it was a matter of "growing up." But in the other cases we have examples of selfishness in what I have called a wrong or false sense. Here there was a centering of concern and interest upon the self which led to lack of attention to the other person. But once again there is a further distinction to be made between what might be styled unconscious or unintentional expressions of selfishness and a willed expression —in the instances I have given, the business was not intended nor even apprehended for what it really was. In a way, that makes it all the more serious, since what we see is a more basic insensitivity to other persons so deep that it is not consciously known to the one who acts in this manner.

It is easy enough to see the failure in or distortion of love shown in this or that particular action. But it is nothing like so simple a matter to grasp the way in which these particular actions disclose a direction of life. They *do* disclose it, however; and the task of the adviser is to help the selfish person to understand that the real problem is not so much in those actions as it is in the more general direction which his life is taking.

The wife in the one case, the husband in the other, were acting in a manner which discloses a tragic fact. Here was the surfacing of a more general movement in existence in which there was a going away from, rather than a moving toward, the reality of love. Doubtless either wife or husband would acknowledge readily enough that in this or that occasion, perhaps during their intimate sexual contacts, there was an instance of wrong relationship, without due consideration of the partner. But to accept the deeper truth about one's own self is very hard indeed. "Oh yes," it might be said, "I was not very generous at that time and I'm sorry for it." Yet this mere acknowledgment is not anything like profound enough. What is acquired is some awareness of the focusing of self on self to the exclusion of others, and as a persistent trend or tendency in which the self's own desires, wants, or needs are so made central that there is little possibility of that wider mutuality or sharing which is integral to love itself. And what makes matters even worse, so often it is true that the very thing which the "guilty" person most wishes is thereby made quite impossible for him. After all, if the argument adduced earlier in this book is correct, what we all really want is to live in love—which is precisely living in a sharing of lives, a give and take, an openness to others and a readiness to receive from them as well as give to them.

It may also be noted that one of the grave dangers faced by a person of homosexual tendency is to be found just here. Granted the goodness of the homosexual desire and drive, these may very well be expressed in a selfish fashion and hence indicate a deeper selfishness—always in our sense of *false* self-concern—which is destructive of the capacity to exist in love. To overcome his loneliness and for other reasons too (not least among them lack of social acceptance), the homosexual man or woman may seek sexual contacts which have no purpose beyond immediate satisfaction or gratification. The other person is then seen merely as a *thing*; and this is a de-personalization of sexuality, to which reference will be made later on. But the contact, which is had regardless of the partner, can have tragic consequences for homosexuals as well as for heterosexuals; and once more I should insist that this is tragic, since in their heart of hearts the homosexuals, like their heterosexual brothers or sisters, are seeking love which will fulfill their total personality and assist the partner to know the same fulfillment. They are not seeking sexual gratification *alone*, although they look for that too and are in no way to be condemned for doing so.

Some years ago I was deeply moved by the way in which a "gay" youth who came to consult me acknowledged that he usually had a (to him) devastating "sense of failure" after what physically had been a "wonderful time" with someone he had picked up for sexual relations. Experience with such "pick-ups" did not give him what he really wanted and desired above all, albeit not always consciously and explicitly. As he said, even with a friend with whom he had been able to establish fairly regular contacts, he had found that while somehow he knew that he wanted to love with his whole self, he had sensed that the actual contacts were likely to be nothing more than physical coupling—good in itself, but not his real desire for union of lives expressed in union of bodies.

On the other hand, both with homosexuals and heterosexuals, a relationship with genuine mutuality, real affection, and a true consideration of the other person, can be (and is) a deeply rewarding and fulfilling experience. Here is the point of such permanence, quasi-permanence,

or attempt at this which is so much more likely to establish precisely that possibility of loving. Lacking this, and
with it lacking also some long-range direction of life in
love, there is also a lack of fulfillment; one is then *not*
moving toward human becoming as a lover-in-the-
making.

Thus we may say that all distortions in sexual expression are basically variations on the theme of false self-
centeredness or selfishness. This is the meaning of the
saying that "selfishness is sin"; where the saying goes
wrong is in its overlooking the necessity for self-concern
in the right sense, such as we saw in the mistaken teaching given the adolescent youth. Nobody is called to be a
"Uriah Heep," the character in Charles Dickens' novel
who seems to invite people to use him as a doormat upon
which they are welcome to trample. That would be the
false kind of humility which leads to disastrous personal loss. Everybody must be concerned for his self both
as a physiological and psychological matter, even if that
concern leads him to "throw himself away" in the service
of others. But all concern for self, if it is to be healthy and
sound, needs to be complemented by an equal concern for
other persons. That is what genuine unselfishness is all
about. It is nothing more nor less than giving *and* receiving, receiving *and* giving; both sides must be accepted if
both parties to the relationship are to grow in love.

To care for others, then, is not the denying of self in
what would amount to masochism at best and to spiritual
or emotional suicide at worst. The "denial of self" which
love involves is a saying "No" to immediate individual-
istic satisfaction, perhaps. It is a dying to a lower and

less genuine level of selfhood in order to bring about the emergence of a higher and more genuine self—and that signifies the "death and resurrection" theme which runs through all Christian thinking and is also present in most deeply humanistic understanding of the true existence of man. In this experience, each helps the other and each brings out the best in the other; unselfishness in one evokes unselfishness in the other.

On the other hand, when somebody is falsely selfish in his relations with another or with others, this produces often enough the sad spectacle of what might be called "induced selfishness" on their side. Not only does the other feel enormous frustration at the beginning. There is also a reaction—as in the case of the husband in my story of the self-centered wife—which tragically makes the partner assert himself in a selfish fashion against the other whose attitude has started the whole business. Many a marriage goes on the rocks because lack of consideration shown by a husband or a wife has provoked a responding lack of consideration. The end product is a cat-and-dog fight, probably conducted with great politeness but nonetheless very damaging to both. In such cases, sexual relations in particular are likely to become what, alas, Jean-Paul Sartre so mistakenly said *all* sexual contacts amount to: a battle in which two persons are each of them seeking to possess, control, and even destroy the other. We may be grateful that Sartre is wrong in thinking that all sexuality amounts to just this; but we can acknowledge that in far too many instances this can be the case. Selfishness breeds selfishness; and the whole enterprise of marriage, as well as the union of two persons of the same gender in a relationship meant to be truly loving, degenerates into a miserable effort at conquest and possession.

In cases of this sort, surely, it is much better to give up altogether than to continue squabbling over who shall possess whom, and how and when. There can be what the present law in Britain calls an "irretrievable breakdown" of the marriage or union; when that happens, some of us are convinced that it is right for the couple to separate, maybe to try again with somebody else. So far as marriage is concerned, Christians are told by the apostle Paul that it is the symbol of "the mystical union of Christ and his church." It does not seem very appropriate to use a cat-and-dog fight, such as I have just described, as that symbol! Unfortunately much in traditional Christian teaching and in the conventional defense of the married state, appears to assume that it *is* thus appropriate.

Of course, everything possible should be done to prevent the destruction of a marriage or union. This is one of the duties of counselors, advisers, confessors, and others who have the "cure of souls." Yet when everything that can be done has been done, there will be plenty of cases where marriages and unions do break down; not always, by any means, but with sufficient frequency to make it imperative for us all—whether Christians or not—to face the possibility and attempt to deal with it. Too much effort to secure the continuance of marriage or union is also to be avoided, for that matter, since excessive effort can produce a bad countereffect. Pastoral wit and wisdom, sympathetic understanding, use of psychiatric and other sorts of help, may be required and may be useful. But there may very well come a point where the break is indeed irretrievable. Then it is better to separate, and it may be right to try again, with somebody else.

Yet the real problem, so far as the persons in the marriage or union are concerned, may remain. John may continue to be falsely self-centered, so that in any and every relationship, even in a new marriage, the same difficulties will reappear. The remedy finally is in a more radical change in John, not simply in a new attempt with another woman. So also with homosexuals. Anybody who has counselled "gay" people knows that so often the basic difficulty is not obviously in either partner to a continuing contact, but in a failure in relationship between them—and thus in something much more serious than the *obvious*. It is the direction of life, the inability or refusal to be aware of the reality of the other, and the often unconscious urge to own or control that other.

In all such cases, the one thing that will be effective is a profound change in personality pattern. And this may come about through a variety of occasions—a tragic incident, a terrible loss, a drastic blow, or at the very best a genuine love which breaks into the hard shell of self-interest and releases the possibilities of giving as well as receiving. As Martin Luther said, man is so often *incurvatus in se*, "twisted in upon himself"; the answer to such a twisting is a "smashing experience," as it were from without, which enables him to see himself for what he is, recognize and acknowledge his failures, relate himself savingly to another or to others, and thus "be saved." When this happens, he is genuinely free to give himself as well as to receive gratefully and humbly from others.

The Scots theologian Chalmers once spoke of "the expulsive power of a new affection." He was talking about the way in which response to the figure of Christ evokes a new capacity to live rightly. This, he said, gives us true liberty and makes us real men. Something of the same sort may happen to anybody who "falls in love," as we put it—and here "falling in love" means exactly the state of being so broken into by another life that false self-centeredness is destroyed and true self-awareness in love is made possible.

Often enough a person who is selfish in the wrong fashion labors under the strange illusion that by being thus and acting thus he is showing himself to be free. Exactly the contrary is true; he is a prisoner to self and the self to which he is prisoner is his lower or false self. He lacks the true freedom which is the capacity to be open to others, to give himself to them, and to receive from them in a gracious manner. To be unable to give oneself is dreadful loss, since it is absence of one aspect of love. On the other hand, to lack the ability to receive from others is equally to lack an aspect of love. Furthermore, if I am to be in the position where I can gladly receive, I have to acknowledge, however vaguely or dimly, that I am in need of something that only another can give me. This is why receiving is so much more difficult than giving, for to receive (and to do this in a gracious manner) is at the same time to acknowledge one's own inadequacy and need. Presumed self-sufficiency is not only a lie but also a preposterous absurdity. To claim self-sufficiency is simply to assert one's self in a wrong and damaging way.

Love's control is to be exercised here. Love requires that we live unselfishly with others. In sexual relationships of whatever variety, where two persons are together in the most intimate union of body, love's control requires that there shall be an equal union of spirit—indeed, a union of the whole personality of each partner with the other. If this does not take place, then the best is not experienced in the sexual contact. And sadly enough, when this best is not known, sought after, moved toward, then—granted all the probable failures along the way—the worse or the worst may come in its place. Selfishness as false self-centeredness is a tragic distortion of love, even a denial of love. Control of sexual expression by love demands an alertness as well as a willed seeking of genuine mutuality.

CRUEL SEXUAL ACTS

Cruelty, in any form, is incompatible with love. It is an expression of an attitude precisely opposite to love. For love is intent upon helping, healing, establishing happiness and joy, whereas cruelty involves physical or mental hurting or harming. And if love is accompanied by anguish, as so often is true, this is not through love's own desire but because anyone who loves—who is profoundly and genuinely in relationship with another, sharing, giving and receiving—must experience both the distress which separation can bring and the pain which comes when the lower self is negated so that the truer self can be affirmed.

Folk wisdom has always known the close association between the ecstacy of love and the anguish of love. It has always seen that love makes demands, not of a self-seeking sort but because the loved one is brought to dedicate and commit himself to the lover, with the suffering that inevitably accompanies such sacrifice of the obvious and immediate in order that the deeper and more ultimate relationship may be given substance. To be living in love is not a matter of "moonlight and roses," nor is it continual "sweetness and light." Love, and living in love, has its hours of darkness.

But the sort of cruelty with which we are here concerned is not that kind of pain, given and received. The Spanish proverb tells us that "to make love is to declare one's sorrows," and William Blake spoke of every act of love as "a little death in the Lord." Here, however, pain is being *inflicted*, gratuitously and needlessly, for the pleasure of the one who inflicts it. And that is a quite different matter.

Such cruelty when found in sexual relations falls into two broad categories, as most of us know. These have come to be called *sadism*, or the inflicting of pain upon others through actions that are cruel or through attitudes that are equally cruel, and *masochism*, or the desire for others to inflict pain, mental or physical, upon oneself. There can be no doubt that a number of men and women derive considerable sensual pleasure if pain is thus physically experienced, or emotional satisfaction if the cruelty is mental in nature. We must accept this as a fact. Yet it is open to question whether it is "normal" for human beings to enjoy sadistic or masochistic acts or attitudes.

Now it is very difficult to define "normalcy." There was, for example, a time when homosexuality was regarded as "abnormal" or "unnatural." Doubtless many people still think that this is the case. Until recently contraception was commonly regarded in the same way and still is so regarded in certain official religious circles. I have met people who would say that "transplants" are wrong because they are "unnatural" or "abnormal." Abortion is very frequently condemned for the same reason, save in those instances where it appears necessary in order to save a life. Most of us would probably dissent from judgments of this sort nowadays: homosexuality would be seen not as "abnormal" but as "different" from the majority's preference; contraception would be accepted as a proper procedure because sexual intercourse is not only for procreation; abortion would be seen as unfortunate but not entirely unnatural; and "transplants" would be considered a very significant and desirable medical advance. But what about pleasure in receiving or inflicting pain? What about sado-masochism in its various forms?

To say that something is "normal" is to say that it is in accordance with the *norm*—in respect to human behavior, that it is to say "agreeable to the proper pattern of human development." Likewise, to call something "natural" is to say that it is "according to nature"—that means, on the human level, in accordance with man's developing or growing toward proper fulfillment. We should be very careful lest we think and talk as if the counting of noses established normalcy or the "natural" way for people to behave. At many times in history the majority have liked or approved of this or that form of activity, which in later ages we have come to regard as improper or wrong. Thus it is necessary to distinguish between what most people approve or accept, on the one hand, and what we may correctly describe as the "normal" or the "natural" for man *as man*. And just here, some basic criterion is required.

In the earlier part of this book, as in my *Making Sexuality Human*, I have urged that this basic criterion is to be found in growth in love. Persons are being created to become lovers; they are a process of development in which the materials they possess and the possibilities which are theirs are meant to be employed in such a fashion that they are more and more adequately a personal agency for love-in-action. And I have argued that this is not only the specifically Christian understanding of human nature but is also intimated in the most profound humanistic interpretation of what it means to be a human being. Therefore I now suggest that the criterion for human normalcy, for "natural" human acts and behavior, will be found just here: does this or that given mode of behavior, does this or that particular act, promote love and help people to become lovers? Or does it work against love and growth in love?

If cruelty, either inflicted upon another or by another, is intent upon hurting or harming, rather than helping and healing, then it is *against* love and constitutes a violation of love's imperative. It is the negation of our basic human criterion; and hence it is *not* "normal," not "natural." Cruelty then is in a different case than homosexuality, contraception, or abortion. As I have urged, the homosexual is different, not deviant; while the practice of contraception can only be taken as "unnatural" if man is reduced to the biological level alone—many of the arguments advanced against contraception turn out to be nothing other than biological, with no attention paid to the specifically human criterion of love. It is true, of course, that sexual intercourse and procreation are associated directly in the biological sphere; yet, as we have seen, man is in a different position from the animals and his technical competence has made possible a further distinction between usual biological consequences of intercourse and the reality of love's expression toward personal union in such intercourse. This is why it is both absurd and inhuman to talk as if it were possible for him to act "naturally" in sexual ways only when his intention is the conception of a child.

The reason for saying that infliction of cruelty and delight in receiving pain are *not* normal or natural is drawn precisely from the specifically human level and rests back upon our definition of what it means *to be human.* I repeat once again, what cannot be said too often, that the entire argument of this book is based on an insistence that to be human is to be on the way to becoming truly a person, while this purpose in becoming human can itself be summed up in the phrase: "on the way to becoming a lover." Love is the criterion of genuine humanity; and whatever negates, denies, or damages love is unnatural and abnormal and in need of what we have been calling the controls exercised by love.

To say this is to say that masochistic and sadistic practices are distortions in sexual expression; they are indeed "perversions" and should be recognized as such. But it should also be clear that in making this statement no judgment is being passed on the *persons* who engage in these practices. They are not usually "wicked"; they are more to be sympathized with, helped, and (so far as may be) enabled to realize that there are better and more fulfilling—because helpful and healing—ways of sexual expression.

Usually, or at least so my own encounters with such people leads me to think, their particular tendency is the result of inadequate, mistaken, or misguided earlier teaching or some experience which titillated them when they were at an impressionable age. One aspect of this problem is found in the excessively masculine and excessively feminine images which for so long have been dominant in our culture. It has been assumed, even taken for granted, that a rough and domineering type of personality is genuinely masculine, so that gentleness, tenderness, and the like are thought to be unmanly. On the other hand, femininity has been associated with a submissive, passive type of personality, so that any positive or clearly affirmative qualities are thought to be improper in a woman. Both these images are mistaken, as we are today aware; perhaps one of the healthy aspects of the present movement toward "unisexuality," as it has been called, is just at this point. Especially among younger people, there is a growing understanding of the truth that genital males may be, even should be, possessed of what used to be thought of as entirely "female" qualities, and vice versa, that genital females may be, even should be, possessed of some supposedly "male" qualities.

Although interest in sado-masochistic practices is found now and again among homosexuals, it would be quite wrong to think that this is generally true. To be sure, a great deal is *said*, in some such circles, about the subject and there are places where male "gays" can engage in these practices as a way in which they can manifest their "dominant male" or "submissive female" personality patterns. But I have just urged that any such precise patterning of personality is a mistake; and I would go on to point out that recent studies have shown the presence of exactly such a sado-masochistic interest in heterosexual circles, even if their expression is a bit more subtle. "I want to be punished": many of us know what that feeling is like; and here again early teaching and experience has much to do with its appearance. Everybody knows that there are marriages in which cruelty, overt or latent, is to be found.

Probably the chief manifestation of sado-masochism is in the subtle attempt to control and use another person, even if this does not lead to actual inflicting of pain as a way of doing so. What is significant in this connection is the direction that a given man or woman is taking. That will be expressed, to greater or lesser degree, in his ways of acting with another in sexual contacts. And here we are not thinking of the "little pains," like "love bites," which may have no serious importance; we are thinking of ways in which one person tries to dominate his partner, even if there may be no overt act of cruelty which would be obvious to any observer.

Two couples with whom I have had consultations illustrate this point. In one case, the husband and wife were to all appearances happily married but certain difficulties arose and in discussion sexual incompatibility was revealed. The husband demanded what he considered his "rights" and he secured them by exerting such pressures on his wife that she was obliged to comply. He did not actually "rape her," to be sure, but he forced her into bed with him when she was unwilling or in poor health and she became ill from his continual requirements. Obviously the husband was acting selfishly but his selfishness was expressed in cruelty. He might just as well have beaten her into utter subjection; instead he put such pressures upon her that she suffered badly in emotional and psychological health. In the other case there was not sadism but masochism. Here too it was the husband who wished to dominate and control, but the wife delighted in being forced into submission. As it turned out, she had become so accustomed to the sort of treatment accorded her that she not only submitted but found a strange satisfaction in being hurt—in this instance physically—whenever the pair were "making love." Of course they were not really "making love" at all, in the true sense of those words; they were enjoying a kind of experience which was quite the opposite of genuine love, one in which the husband was able to assert his latent cruelty and the wife to enjoy the pain she suffered. In each case, the best that an adviser could do was to help the partners understand that their acts were manifestations of something more radically wrong with their lives and the direction which those lives was taking—away from, not toward, realizing the expression of true love.

We are told that human beings have an "inbuilt aggressiveness," as Dr. Anthony Storr has called it in his book *Aggression.*[1] Conversation with some colleagues in the University of Cambridge, themselves expert in animal and human behavior patterns, has led me to think that "aggression" is the wrong word to use for something which indeed is very genuinely human, namely, the inbuilt assertive quality of human personality. We have already spoken of the need for the right sort of "self-centeredness." So here too we can see the entire propriety of the right sort of assertiveness. Without it, nobody could hope to survive. Without some such self-assertion, as without some proper self-centeredness, human integrity could not be maintained; my scientific colleagues tell me that every animal, and man as also in this respect an animal, must possess the capacity to "stand up for himself." But this need not be expressed in an anti-social way since (as my friends have also pointed out) cooperation

[1] Anthony Storr, *Aggression* (Baltimore: Penguin Books, 1970).

and the common life are equally essential to survival. In other words, not aggression but self-assertion is all right in itself, provided it does not get out of hand and try to run roughshod over others—when it does that, it becomes dangerous to society and *also* damaging to personality. In a similar fashion, a certain degree of submissiveness is good and proper for persons and will help in their sound development, since we must live together, accept one another, and be prepared to accommodate ourselves to those with whom we are placed. But such self-submissiveness can also be exaggerated; and instead of a healthy readiness to give others their due and hence to respect and value their rights, it can be turned into the "walk on me, please" attitude (as a friend phrased it) to life's demands and to those with whom we have to do. Then it too becomes damaging to personality.

In sum, we may agree that love is never a business of coercion nor of cruelty. It is tenderness, gentleness, kindness; and yet it is without false humility or debilitating submissiveness. It is enormously strong; but its strength is not in sheer force but in persuasion which is not the "hidden" variety of which Vance Packard has written but rather the genuine persuasion which is concerned with awakening and strengthening the best in others, so that true mutuality may be found. So soon as cruelty appears in human contacts, above all in those of an explicitly genital or physical sort, something is shown to be radically wrong in the depths of human motivation. The movement toward realization of potential manhood as love-in-action is inhibited or reversed. Likewise, when submissiveness shows itself in an exaggerated way, the same indication is given.

William James wrote a famous essay on "the moral equivalent of war," urging that we find ways in which assertiveness could be channeled in noncoercive and nonbelligerent fashion, thus serving socially acceptable and useful ends. Much the same suggestion might be made about the ordinary self-assertiveness of people, to avert dangerous aggression, and about the ordinary and natural submissiveness of persons to authority or to other persons, to avert dangerous masochistic tendencies. Cruelty in itself is a distortion; it is in need of control by love. What is back of the urge to assert self or to submit self to others can have a good and healthy expression. Cruelty as sadism can be transformed into vigor of character which hurts nobody; cruelty as masochism can be transformed into an acceptance of others which does not delight in being hurt or controlled by them but still finds satisfaction in receiving as well as giving.

Such a transformation can be effected by love itself. But the way in which this is done is by opening human personality to the reality of the human situation— which means, in effect, to other persons as companions on life's journey and moving together with oneself toward fulfillment in loving. We must be ready to let love take over. Without such readiness, very little can be accomplished in transforming aggression or submission; with it, coercion and cruelty can be overcome and healthy self-assertion and self-denial given their proper place. A man or woman who knows that he or she has a tendency toward sadism or masochism can see to it that situations are avoided where practices of this sort—or their latent emotional equivalent—are given opportunity. The man or woman can also see to it that they decide, in the freedom which is part of human personality, to open their lives to the influx of love from others.

Here, more plainly than in many other areas, is the significance of the "expulsive power of a new affection," to which we referred earlier. When somebody has really "fallen in love," however this may have occurred, he is delivered both from the urge to control by cruel force and from the urge to be trampled on. He is delivered from the former because the only power exerted by him will be in the persuasion of love itself; he is delivered from the latter because love is above all (as our next section will show) a personalizing influence by virtue of which we can stand on our feet and know that we are important simply because we are loved by another.

None of this is easy; but then nothing worthwhile in human life is easily attained. Effort is required to open oneself to love and to a lover; yet in the last analysis, one is the recipient of a gift which one has not earned through one's own effort. Love is always "of grace," never "of works." This does not mean, however, that we have nothing to do. Here is the strange paradox in human loving just as we have here also the paradox in the divine-human relationship. As Paul put it, "Work out your own salvation with fear and trembling. For it is God [or may I say love] which worketh in you both to will and to do of his good pleasure (Phil. 2:12-13, KJV)."

SEXUAL CONTACTS LACKING
PERSONAL RELATIONSHIPS

Human beings are not things; they are not fixed entities; they are not machines. They are persons-in-the-making. Every man, woman, or child is an "I," with self-identity which gives him his distinctive quality; he is related with other men, women, and children, as "I" to "thou" or "I" to "you." Furthermore, he is on the move, or "becoming" what potentially he "is," namely, a lover who is being created "toward the image of God," the supreme and cosmic Lover. So we have maintained in this book. And love is always a personalizing agency; it not only sees the beloved "other" as a person but it is effectual in developing the other's personality to a higher degree.

We see this personalizing quality in the way in which family affection leads to growth. A child knows and experiences the affection of his parents and his brothers and sisters. Psychologists tell us that this is how the child becomes a self-conscious, free, responding, open being. An unloved child will grow up hard, suspicious, closed in upon himself with little if any capacity for trust and confidence. He will be "lonely and afraid," as a poem puts it. For without affection from family and later from friends, growth is inhibited in tragic ways. Doubtless many of us have seen this happen and have been appalled by the stunting, twisting, or frustrating of personal development. Here love is the clue to human living; it is the way in which we are enabled to "become" our true selves, moving toward maturity as men.

When human beings are treated as *things*, the possibility of mutuality is denied them. You cannot be in a "give-and-take" relationship with an object. But when human beings are treated humanly, such relationships are in the center of the picture. Obviously the most intimate "I-thou" cannot exist with everyone we happen to meet. But the important question is whether the contacts which we do have are, first of all, *toward* personal relationships rather than kept on the "thing" level; and second, are *of the sort* that from them and in them there is the material out of which deepening awareness may grow.

Nowhere is this so obvious as in the physical expression of love in human sexuality. In these contacts of a physical sexual nature, it is always possible to act in such a manner that *im*personality is being asserted. The husband can treat his wife simply as if she were a thing for him to use, sexually speaking; the wife can treat her husband as if he were but an object who gives her satisfaction. In homosexual relations the same may be the case; indeed, we might remark that one sad consequence of social rejection of homosexuals (especially male homosexuals) is that they feel driven to such impersonal contacts—I am thinking of what must often go on between the man who has "picked up" another because there was no other way for him to rid himself of loneliness or find release from sexual pressures, and the person whom he has thus secured even if that person was willing to be "used." The word used is significant, since nobody can ever "use" a person or one whom he is treating in a genuinely personal manner; he can only "use" a *thing*, and in such instances the person then becomes just that and nothing more. In both the heterosexual and the homosexual instances, a machine of some sort might serve just as well, perhaps even better!

On the other hand, loving contacts of a sexual sort can be splendid in their affirmation of personality and in their promotion of genuine personal growth. And honesty compels us also to acknowledge that sometimes what has begun as a "thing" relationship may become something much more personal; a man or woman may find himself truly "in love" with the other, although it did not begin in that way at all. This is one of those remarkable possibilities of which love can, and sometimes does, take advantage.

I have quoted elsewhere, but think worth repeating here, an incident in James Baldwin's novel *Giovanni's Room*,[2] where David, the young American homosexual, tells his Italian friend Giovanni that he knows very well "*what* you want." Giovanni replies, "It's you who talk about *what* I want. For me it's *whom* I want." The incident has to do with a homosexual contact, of course; but the principle which it enunciates is applicable to human loving of every sort. In those words we have a beautifully succinct statement of the centrality of personality in right human loving: "not *what* but *whom*." At the same time we have a poignant reminder of the

[2] James Baldwin, *Giovanni's Room* (New York: Dial, 1956).

way in which something very different indeed can be substituted for that personal and personalizing quality —the ultimately unsatisfying, certainly damaging, use of another as if he or she were but an object that happens to be at hand.

For most members of the human race, the estate of matrimony is the situation in which interpersonal relationships are realized sexually or physically. The context of the married state, its approval by society, its legal sanctions, and its long historical development toward monogamy, combine to make it an ideal condition for the establishment of "I-thou" at its highest and best. In marriage, the sexual union of husband and wife is expressive of their mutual love and provides what I have styled the physiological-psychological basis upon which that love can build. The very permanence which is expected in marriage helps in this process, since it provides opportunity for continuing deep affection not so much in spite of but precisely because of the disagreements, conflicts, and vicissitudes which the couple share together.

For those who are not heterosexual in temperament, there is an approximation to this same sort of enduring union when two persons of the same sex undertake living together with mutual affection, finding in their sexual contacts the grounding for the love they have one for the other. This is not a marriage in the historical meaning of the word and it is unfortunate that sometimes that word is used for such unions. But as in marriage, such permanence as can be managed will help the growing together; and this is why counselors ought to do all in their power to assist homosexuals to achieve such a continuing union. Despite social pressure and condemnation, many in fact do achieve it; and they are people whom we all ought to admire.

Somehow, it seems, the human race has been moving through its history toward as much permanence as can be attained between those who care deeply for each other. I suspect that the reason is that the almost unconscious wisdom of the race has seen that personal development, indeed the development *of* personality, is best secured in this way. Now it is plain enough that such permanence or quasi-permanence demands that there shall be a commensurate sense of mutual responsibility—and about this we shall have much to say in the following section. For the moment, however, let us stress that only when sexuality has this personalizing quality can those who express it physically "stick together" spiritually and emotionally as they are joined together in an explicitly genital manner. That explains why one of the controls exercised by love, as the reference for and the criterion of human sexuality, is found precisely at this point.

We might put it this way: *love forbids impersonal sexual behavior.* Obviously love does not make such behavior impossible, as we know very well. My point is simply that when love *is* present, the impersonal is ruled out, at least in principle. Naturally there can be much in sexual intercourse which seems almost automatic once a beginning has been made. But this appearance is deceptive. The automatic or quasi-automatic is taken up into the personal and becomes instrumental

for the expression of the personal. Despite the little
manuals that sometimes describe sexual acts as if they
were to be merely a matter of "good technique," the
truth of the matter is that love is really an *art* and that
its sexual expression is an art too. As in art, there is a
spontaneity, a freshness, an openness, an unexpected
novelty, all of which are *not* mechanical in nature, even
if there are mechanical aspects and techniques which
will help to perfect the art form.

The evil in prostitution is just here. For as we noted
above, the relationship between a prostitute and his or
her "customer" by its very nature is a matter of thing,
not person. The prostitute is paid for performing a
"service" or providing a desired "article"; and it has
been said, in memoirs written by prostitutes and in
studies of their style of life and activity, that in most
cases they do not want, perhaps even fear, a more intimate kind of relationship, or, shall we say, one that
puts the performance of the sexual genital act in a
wider context of a personal sort. Of course, there are
exceptions here. One thinks of the film *Never on Sunday*, where gentleness and concern shown by a prostitute enable a young sailor to be secure in his sexuality
after a period of fear and uncertainty. Or again, there
is the male prostitute portrayed by Joe d'Alessandro in
Andy Warhol's film *Flesh*. In this moving film the
young man tries hard not only to give "satisfaction" to
his clients but also to be genuinely friendly with them,
difficult as this sometimes turns out to be. But I think
that in the majority of cases what is portrayed in these
two films is rather unlikely. This makes the prostitute

a sad spectacle; such a person is in the horrible position of being "de-personalized" at the central point where possible life in love is available.

Probably one reason for the apparently odd fact that many female prostitutes seem to be lesbians, who can genuinely love only one of their own gender, is related to the way in which heterosexual love has been thus depersonalized for them. What can be said about the male prostitute I do not know, although it has been pointed out that he often insists that he is not himself "gay" but only engages in the business for money, preferring meaningful sex with a female. Evidence seems to go against this however; reports by experts tell us that most male prostitutes are deluding themselves or trying to delude others when they deny their own homosexual inclination. In any event, prostitution of either sort is almost an "organized" drive against the control of sexual contacts by love as the point of reference and criterion. That is why it is such an unfortunate and inhuman business.

In putting this so bluntly, I do not intend to engage in facile condemnation of the prostitute as a human being, however much I deprecate her or his practices. Usually people are forced into prostitution, sometimes as a way for escaping from a difficult family, sometimes for lack of other work, often because it appears an "easy" way to earn money and very often because of personality defects of one sort or another. They are to be helped, not condemned, even if their "profession" cannot be commended. Much the same should be said about their "clientele," who so frequently are men who seem unable to find relief from loneliness, who want some simulation of affection and who seek an opportunity to do something about their sexual desires and pressures. I should also wish to suggest that the hidden motivation, hidden certainly from the conscious thought of such men, is a yearning for *real* love, although they do not know how to find it and very likely would experience great anguish if they were actually given it— it would be in such contrast with, and stand in such unspoken judgment upon the cheap and readily obtainable substitutes.

In each section of this chapter I have tried to give an illustration or two. For impersonal or depersonalized sexual contacts I can provide one which seemed to me tragic in the extreme. Many years ago I knew a young man, about my age, who was frightened of all relationships in which he himself might be seriously involved and hence be forced to make a commitment. Just what had brought him to that sorry state I do not know; but some of us who knew him felt that he was a pathetic person—attractive in appearance, brilliant in intellect, wanting very much to be devout, able to be scintillating in conversation, yet "scared" of any relationship which brought him very close to another.

With this sort of pattern of existence the only possible sort of sexual release he seemed able to find was either in masturbation, which did not satisfy him since he had some deep sense, or so it appeared, that he *ought* to be able to relate to another human being, or else in the use of a paid prostitute with whom he could simulate intimacy without ever actually experiencing it.

How many people there are like this I do not know; but certainly there must be a considerable number of them among us. What this young man needed was some affection which would break into his self-imposed isolation. It did not happen, to my knowledge; and the last time that I heard about him he was well into a frustrated middle age. I wish him well and I hope that there is still time for something to happen to him which will release him from his bondage and into personal relations.

One happier instance, this time having to do with marital relationships, comes to mind. Here the husband had been a frequent visitor to prostitutes in his early years and later had found women who were easy to "make," as the saying goes. In all these contacts, however, there had been no *real* interpersonal sharing, only the release of sexual desire on his part. And then he fell in love, head-over-heels in love, with a charming girl whom he married. But his past experience had been such that after the first raptures of their honeymoon, his approach and behavior in intercourse was purely mechanical. He found himself wanting a sexual contact; he was excited physically; he used his wife as if she were there just as a thing to receive into her his genital organ; and then he turned over on his back and went to sleep.

Naturally she found this kind of intercourse more than frustrating; it was as if *she* were not really there at all. Hence it was worse than if he had obviously been a selfish or cruel person. He was neither; he was just incapable of recognizing the necessary personal quality of significant sexual union. But the wife was a wise and

loving woman. She finally persuaded her husband to go
with her to talk things over with a counselor. Wonder-
fully enough, it was as if a miracle had taken place.
Once the business was "laid on the table" and frankly
discussed between them in the presence and with the
help of the counselor, the husband saw the point. He
became quite different in his sexual contacts. Here *was*
a case where love had broken in, through the concern
of his wife and her determination, not only that she
should be treated personally, but in her recognition that
her husband needed frankness and objectivity if he were
also to come to an understanding of person-to-person
sex.

This brings us back, once again, to the theme of this
book. Love has its controls in respect to sexual behavior; and if only they can be grasped, appreciated,
and then applied, quite astounding things can happen.
Love, in its finest sense, is very wise and knows how to
act in situations where most other remedies would fail
or have failed.

IRRESPONSIBLE SEXUAL BEHAVIOR

I like the story that Nels Ferré told in his little book
Making Religion Real. When Ferré was a graduate stu-
dent at Harvard under Alfred North Whitehead, one
day he was having a consultation with the famous
Anglo-American philosopher and he ventured to put to
his teacher a question which Ferré himself calls "naïve":
How would you "characterize reality, in one sentence"?
The philosopher was "taken aback at such a boyish
question," Ferré wrote. But after a few minutes thought

he answered it in six words: "It matters, and it has consequences."[3]

Consequences. We have already spoken of the plain truth that the world is made up of events which have consequences. Something happens bringing the past to a focus possessed of some novel possibility; and *then* the new occasion perishes, comes to an end, is finished in and of itself. But its influence, its results, its effects upon what comes afterward persist. That is the way the world goes. And that is the way human life goes too. There is no escape from the process.

At levels below the human the consequences cannot be consciously thought about; at the human level they can. We know they will happen; we do not know *how* they will happen, in any detail, nor do we always see just *what* they are going to be—far from it! But we are nonetheless responsible, through the decisions which we as "large-scale organisms" have made, for those consequences. That is part of what is meant when we venture to think about ourselves as "moral beings."

Now in an older moral theology, it used to be said that "he who wills an act, wills its consequences, whether they are the results which are intended or are the incidental, even accidental ones, that accompany what is directly purposed." There is truth here with which we must reckon, even if the statement of it seems somewhat exaggerated—for how can you be held responsible, in any truly serious sense, for what you had

[3] Nels F. S. Ferré, *Making Religion Real* (New York: Harper & Bros., 1955), p. 26. Used by permission.

no intention whatsoever of having come to pass? Yet in a way you *are* responsible, for had you not decided that way, such and such would not have taken place at all.

We need not explore here all the ramifications of this somewhat complicated problem of responsibility. Suffice it to say that precisely because we are human, possessed of rationality, able to make significant free decisions, and living in a world in which everything is interconnected or interrelated, one of the marks of our human nature is willingness to *accept* responsibility for decisions made and for what they bring about. And in no area of experience is this so obvious to a person of integrity as in the realm of sexual experience. To relate this to our main argument, let us say that one of love's controls is the insistence that irresponsible sexual behavior is not fully human; it denies one of love's imperatives and reduces man from his status as a "lover-in-the-making" to that of the beasts.

Few things are more depressing, often more terrifying, than the spectacle of irresponsible sexuality. I recall how even I and my fellow-students, half a century ago, were horrified by one of our classmates who admitted, even boasted, again and again that he was "out to get all he could get" whenever he had a "date" (although in those days we did not talk that way) with a girl. He did not care for *her*; he felt no sense of responsibility about *her*, although he did care about himself and hence always had in his pocket a contraceptive device so that *he* would not be open to blame for the conception of a child. He went about like an animal in search of his prey, and that was that. We were not particularly ideal-istic young men, but we felt that our friend was altogether too lacking in fundamental moral sense—and so he was.

But it is not simply the possible consequence of an unwanted child that should inspire responsibility. After all—and especially now in the day of "the pill" and much more knowledge about such matters—that kind of consequence is fairly readily avoided. The really unfortunate consequences are what happens to somebody's personality when she is treated in this cavalier fashion. I know quite well that some will say that nowadays "girls ask for it." That may be true, sometimes, but it is no reason for responding to this supposed invitation without regard for them and their well-being.

I trust it will be understood that I am not at this point arguing for absolute rejection of all pre-marital sexual experimentation, as it is called, nor suggesting that young people may not be drawn to and find good in sexual contacts which are wanted by both parties and which in any event are nowadays usually taken for granted as part of the life of adolescents and young adults. There are other considerations in these matters about which I wrote in my earlier book. I am only giving an illustration of how irresponsibility can be a most undesirable aspect of such sexual expression.

The real question to be asked, then, is whether a man or woman, boy or girl, realizes and accepts as part of the controls in sexual behavior, the consequences in total personal growth which are for the good or for the less good, or even for the bad. And incidentally, I find that young people today, despite their supposed laxity, are much more prepared to see and assume responsibility than many of their elders. The notion that they "jump into any bed at any time," as an acquaintance of mine once put it, is a malign lie. In *Making Sexuality Human* I cited a phrase used by a young undergraduate: "permissiveness, with affection and responsibility"; and I am convinced that this is found much more frequently than older people think.

The consequences are not only those which affect the person himself. More important than that, they are those that have to do with the other person or persons in the situation. They are also the less obvious but diffused results of *anything* one does in an interpenetrative world. I say "less obvious" because much of the time there is simply no way of observing these consequences. They are hidden deep in the lives of others; they are effective in producing or tending to produce new types of situations in which the contribution of any single individual seems trivial; and they are often long range in their chain of effects. That they *do* have results or fruits is unquestionably the case, however; and to whatever degree is possible for us they must be taken into account if we are to act responsibly.

In this connection, also, there is the business of "promise making" and "promise keeping." In human relationships this is highly important; we are constantly saying, with every appearance of *meaning* it, that we will do this or that. What then happens? Do we in fact do what we have said we would do? In the intimacy of sexual life, especially as this is known in marriage, in the "engagement" which precedes marriage, and in other kinds of union of lives as well, "promising" is an integral part of the total picture. This is symbolized in the promises made at a wedding, by both parties who there undertake a common life in mutual support and help until they die. A practical consequence of such promises is the exertion of every effort to maintain that life together. We have seen that this may be impossible despite strong effort; but until failure is plainly demonstrable the control of love indicates that the promise should be kept. One could perhaps say (with reliance on the available evidence) that marriages "break down" more often from irresponsibility in keeping promises of mutual help and support than from any other single cause. One of the partners, maybe both, simply cannot bring himself to realize that marriage is not always "fun"; there is work involved in any union of lives and this requires patience as well as courage and loyalty. The sequence of marriage-divorce-remarriage-divorce, all too familiar to us, is not a pretty sight. It amounts often to polygamy *seriatim*, as I have heard it phrased, and the cause is more often than not irresponsibility in keeping promises, with the results in distrust and insecurity that this irresponsibility may very well bring about.

This consideration of responsibility—if you will, of duty in respect to human sexual relations and their physical concomitant—is often taken to be a denial of the delightful spontaneity which should characterize life, not least sexual life. To think in this fashion is a mis-

take, however. A completely disordered existence is
almost certainly bound to lead to dissatisfaction and
harm; we shall have more to say about this in the next
section of this chapter. But its contrary, an ordered
existence, in no sense suggests that within a broad area
of order and with an inclusive sense of responsibility
for maintaining that order, there is no opportunity for
the freshness, unexpectedness and novelty of expression
which give all of us our delight in loving. Talk of con-
jugal "rights," meaning the right to the other's body, is
a poor way of saying what is here in mind. In a marriage
where love is utterly central—that is, where husband
and wife are always giving and receiving, supporting
and helping each other, sharing the totality of existence
with one another this "freshness" is bound to be present; and what some would call "rights" become priv-
ileges. The joy of giving when the other desires, like
the joy of receiving when the other gives—and often
enough when one partner is not feeling very keenly the
wish to receive or to give—is made possible precisely
because the total relationship is such that this *physical*
willingness is based upon an overall *psychological* willingness that in its turn is grounded in an overall *personal* willingness. This is why it is often a good thing
for a couple to talk frankly, as unemotionally as possible, and with absolute sincerity, about the "wants"
and the "needs" of each, sexually speaking.

I remember that my mother was rather horrified when
a niece told her that she had been talking in this fashion
with the young man whom she was soon to marry. That

was a long time ago and very likely my cousin was a bit in advance of her time. Today, however, we should agree that what she was doing was the right thing—it was a way of getting the matter of responsibility straight at the start. Things might change, to be sure; but at least that couple knew each other better and hence could adjust to each other with more adequacy.

Finally, we return to the theme of direction or movement of life. The sense of responsibility is not given us all at once; like everything else it grows from small beginnings. The decisions made from day to day, tiny as they may seem to be, are the necessary material from which such a sense takes its rise. As we decide, on this and that particular occasion, to act as responsibly as we can, looking at the probable consequences of our act, the direction we are taking will become clearer and our later decisions will also become much easier; indeed, sometimes they will not seem like decisions at all, but simply the obvious thing under the circumstances. Further, we are to judge others more by this general direction in which they are seen to be moving than by a given instance or moment in the relationship. I have stressed time and again this matter of the general direction of life; it becomes increasingly important in my own thinking about all moral issues which have to do with persons and their common existence. But nowhere is this so clear—to me anyway—as in the sexual pattern of life for men and women and in their behavior as sexual beings. Love's controls have this processive movement in view; this is why they can be both demanding in content *and* generous in application.

INORDINATE SEXUALITY

A famous saying of Augustine asks that God will "order [his] loving"; and in the Middle Ages sin was regularly defined as *inordinatio*, "disorder." This was a way of indicating that moral wrong is primarily a matter of a *good thing* gone wrong, not of an evil that is radical in the sense that it is at the very roots of human nature as such. I am convinced that this insight was both profound and correct—otherwise we should have to hold to a doctrine of "total depravity" in a sense that even John Calvin did not intend.

At its *roots*, human nature is "all right," so to say, because it is created by God who cannot make evil. In its concrete expressions, however, there is a failure to preserve the ordered pattern which God purposes, where every element and aspect is so related to every other, and where all are so held together by a dominant motivation ("purity of heart" or single-mindedness), that human existence is healthy and sound. When any one element or aspect gets attention or expression out of proportion to the total pattern, things fall apart—or otherwise phrased, human personality is distorted. This approach seems to me to be of great help in understanding what thoughtful people can mean when they use the word "sin"; above all, it can help us when we are thinking of our vocation to become lovers, how this can be misdirected, and how in sexual behavior it can manifest itself in ways that harm and damage.

The point is that you *can* have "too much of a good thing." For if any *one* good thing is given exclusively or absolutely central place, the pattern of life is dis-

turbed and what in itself is good becomes *bad for you.*
Perhaps we can all think of illustrations of this principle.
Religion is a good thing, shall we say? But when somebody devotes all of himself to it and disregards everything else, it becomes obsessive. Then we have the
spectacle of religion made into an end in itself. All other
human interests and concerns are subordinated to it and
the result is a deadly and monotonous existence. Baron
Friedrich von Hügel used to warn that a religiously
minded person had desperate need of secular interests
if his religion was not to go sour. "Grace needs nature
to work on," as he put it. In many other areas we can
see the same "inordination"—the man of affairs who is
nothing but that; the politician who sees everything in
terms of maneuvering people to support his party or
platform; the woman who is so much a "house body"
that she cannot envisage anything else; even the scientist who is *only* a scientist with no time for wider human
interests and contacts.

Now in matters of sexual existence the same may
take place. Sex in its physical expression may become
the whole *of* life; and that is surely a weird obsession,
resting back upon a complete misunderstanding of the
genuine meaning of sex's centrality *in* human life. That
way, we may say, lies ultimate madness. Sigmund Freud
has been seriously misjudged at this point. What the
great father of psychoanalysis said was that sex is
central to all that man is and does; he did *not* say that
in itself it constituted that totality. It is too bad that
those who have but slight knowledge of his work so
unfairly condemn him. For sex *is* central; and I suggest

that one of the ways in which its true centrality can be lost is by obsessively devoting all one's time and interest to it. That is to lose right proportion on the subject.

It is natural and inevitable, for example, that an adolescent moving from puberty toward maturity should focus much of his attention on his sexual desires and drives. This is the way in which he discovers himself physiologically and psychologically. When an *adult* thus focuses his attention on that one thing only, he is hardly showing himself properly mature. Alas, there are many men, perhaps even a not inconsiderable number of women too, who seem never to have grown up in this respect. They are rather trying people to be with since they so often assume that everybody else is like them. In such cases a good thing, indeed a very good thing (which sexuality most certainly is), has become a bad thing precisely because it has been given a disproportionate place in the totality of our existence.

But love is not in the same case, for nobody can ever love too much. The wisdom of the race, secular and religious, knows this very well. Yet love's controls tell us that in expressing itself, love always tries to be as "ordinate"—patterned and in right proportions—as it is possible for it to be. In sexual behavior of an overt sort this is patently meant to be true, which is why we sometimes wonder if those who are (to use the word once more) "obsessed" by sex can truly know and experience love. Doubtless they can, but their capacity must be seriously reduced.

Yet we should be unjust if we forgot the point made earlier—that even in distorted expressions of sex, there still remain both its necessity as the basis for human love and also the fact that such distortions and exaggerations and twistings do not and cannot deny that the essential drive of all persons, by virtue of their being human, is toward love. We cannot emphasize this often enough nor strongly enough; to lose sight of it is to reduce humans to the level of animals or even lower.

Some years ago I met a pleasant young man who seemed at first acquaintance to be entirely balanced or adjusted. But I soon discovered that any conversation one had with him arrived sooner or later at sex. There was nothing obscene in what he said; the trouble was that after a while those who knew him got very bored. Was this his *one* interest in life? It seemed so, not that he acted much upon it so far as one could tell. I felt that what he needed was some compelling interest which would occupy his time and attention, rather like another and older friend who told me that he too had been obsessed by the matter until he discovered, oddly enough, that a study of the varieties of interpretations of *Hamlet* interested him rather more! Perhaps it does not much matter what is the interest which will balance an excessive sexual focus, so long as it will secure that sex is not taken to be the only thing that matters in life.

We have all met the man who is unable to keep from telling "dirty stories." Sometimes they are genuinely funny and in that case worth telling. Often they are only delight in "dirt" for its own sake; and this is pathetic. A clergyman whom I once met was of this sort. Outwardly he was clean-cut and seemed devoted to his calling; but one could only conclude that his mind was like a cesspool if his continual story telling was any clue. And this again was pathetic.

In marriage, and in sexual unions between homosexuals, the same obsession can sometimes be seen in actual behavior. Sexual relations are important and good, to be sure; and any marriage or union where they are lacking is far from being a total sharing of lives. On the other hand, if that is *all* that seems important, something has gone wrong with the relationship itself or it never was a union of lives, only a wish to unite bodies and stop there. Some months ago a pleasant young man came to consult me about his future. He had heard that I was sympathetic to homosexuals and felt that I would understand his situation. What it boiled down to was this. He had lived for five years with another young man who he had thought was very much in love with him as he was with his friend. But it turned out that the love was all on *his* side; the other man was simply interested in him for physical relations. The significant moment in our conversation was when he said to me, "I wanted our whole selves to be united and I found that only our genitals were."

What that young man said can often be said with equal truth in respect to the marriage of a man and a woman. The relationship looked as if it were truly one of love, in the fullest sense of sharing between the partners; it has turned out to be only a superficial union of lives and primarily desire for coition. What ought to be central as the expression of love has become exclusively the point of the relationship. Thus as a relationship it is not full and complete; love is being rejected, denied, or harmed, if it is there at all.

Surely I need not elaborate further. Love's controls are such that they require proportion and rightful ordering in everything. Whatever may be said for or against sex *without* love in any given circumstance, most of us would agree that the truly human expression of sexuality is *in love*. This is what was meant by the comment made earlier, that there is a genuine difference between "making love" and "having sex." The latter can be gratifying but is it *as* gratifying as the former? And if it is not, why is this? I suggest that the reason is to be found in what I have styled disproportion, sexuality in an inordinate mode or manifestation.

It comes down, then, to harmonious or (to revert to Dr. Fosdick's much-criticized word) "beautiful" ways in which our human sexuality can show itself in action. Nor is that far from the view in the gospels. Jesus' attitude toward sex, so far as we can gather, was the typical Jewish one. Sex was good, God-given, and for most people—if not for Jesus himself, and about this we have no information but it *seems* that he felt called to a nonmarried life in order to carry out his demanding vocation—it was to be both accepted and enjoyed in marriage. But Jesus warned against "lust," as the Authorized Version translates it. "Lust" in this context does not mean ordinary sexual desires; it means *"inordinate"* sexual desire *and* act. That is why "the man who looks at a woman to lust after her, commits adultery with her in his heart." That man's difficulty is that he is obsessed by the matter and cannot even see a person of the other

sex without "wanting her" physically. Since he cannot
secure this, he "wants her" "in his heart."

I urge that this is not the way to true human satisfaction. It may be pleasant enough for a time; but who of
us has seen a roué, a sexually satiated person, without
feeling sorry for him? He has so tragically missed the
mark. He has lost the deepest value in sexual contacts
because he has taken them out of their best context and
made them the one thing in life for which he strives.
Even so, he is fooling himself. For deeper than his consciously known physical want there is another, and very
wonderful want: it is the desire for love, for life in
shared love, and for joy in the giving and receiving which
it includes. But having lost his way, neglected the culti-
vation of this capacity for love and focused everything
on physical contact alone, he reminds one of George
Santayana's definition of a fanatic as "the man who
redoubles his efforts when he has forgotten his aim."

The *aim* of human life is to grow into manhood as a
lover-in-the-making. To forget that is to miss everything.
And this, I take it, is why one of love's most significant
controls has to do with rejecting inordinate sexual
behavior.

At this point, it may be useful to introduce some comments about what is nowadays styled "pornography,"
for while this is not a matter of overt sexual contacts it
is closely related to the sexual side of life and may have
its effect upon those contacts. Nobody doubts that there
has been an enormous increase in the amount of explicit
sexual content in theater, cinema, art, and literature,
these days. Some would say that the whole business is

evil and should be suppressed, if necessary by legal action against those who "offend." I believe, however, that we should make some distinctions here.

I take it that there is a difference between showing and writing about sex and its manifestations, on the one hand, and a vulgar obsession with these on the other. The adjective vulgar gets at the essential issue. When I saw the well-known theatrical production *O Calcutta*, I was struck by two things. First, there was the breathtaking beauty of some of the dances, done completely in the nude, and there was the genuine humor of some of the skits which were included. For much of the time the actors and actresses were indeed nude, often the jokes were lewd, and sometimes they were rude. It is obvious that I am playing with words here for I want to go on to say that my general impression was that much of the show was, in the second place, *crude*. That was all I could find to object to.

On the other hand, there was a fine play produced in London two years ago: *The Changing Room* by David Storey. This was a half-documentary, portraying the periods before and after a football match by a professional team; and it was set in what in the United States would be called the locker room of the clubhouse. During both episodes all the players were entirely naked at one time or another. But there was not the slightest suggestion of *crudity* in the presentation; it was, as I have said, almost a "documentary" of one afternoon in a professional team's season. Yet some defenders of "purity" were scandalized by the play—absurdly, I thought. Simi-

larly, the depiction of love-making with sexual overtones
and sometimes explicit sexual activity, especially in films
(I think of the film made of Lawrence's *Women in Love*,
for one thing, and of Pasolini's delightful rendition of
Boccaccio's *Decameron*, on the other), can be either
natural and right, or crude and vulgar. Both films mentioned are in the former class, to my mind.

Much the same may be said about fiction. Here, to
bring the matter to a very clear focus, I mention two
novels dealing with explicit homosexual relationships.
One of them is the reticent yet frank posthumously
published novel *Maurice* by my old friend and one-time
associate in Cambridge, E. M. Forster. Forster did not
publish the novel during his lifetime because both when
he wrote it (in the first decade of this century) and for
some years afterward, the subject was taboo. I doubt if
many people today were shocked by the two or three
incidents in which sexual contacts were hinted at. A contemporary novel which also treats of homosexuality is
The Lord Won't Mind by Gordon Merrick. In this novel
the sexual contacts of Peter and Charlie are described
with no attempt to be other than forthright and explicit.
The words used to describe what goes on between them
are the ordinary common words for such acts and the
acts themselves as described by the author leave little to
the imagination. Yet the total impression the book gives
is not in any sense obscene; or so I thought as I finished
it. The explicit sex was in the context of a love, tenderness, and sharing of life which made it seem entirely
natural. I should say the same about such a book as

James Baldwin's moving novel *Another Country,* where both heterosexual and homosexual acts are described.

On the other hand, there are plenty of books in which the author appears to set out with the single purpose of titillating the reader—I give no titles for I do not wish to advertise the books! And the real pornography in these books is in what I have called vulgarity and crudity, not in the sexual descriptions as such but in the leering way in which (as it seems) the writer is talking about them.

All of which is to say that we have here still another instance of disorder or inordination, where things are not seen in a natural and healthy perspective but where much effort is expended in putting sexual life *out of context*. In other words, there is obsession with explicit sexual activity of a genital sort with no interest in, no awareness of, and no desire to help the audience or readers grasp something of the wonder, glory, and splendor of human sexuality. I advocate no censorship, for that can be frightening in its possible results. What I *do* urge is sensitivity among readers and by audiences; responsibility by writers, playwrights, and producers; and good taste on all sides.

While working on this book, I have received a fascinating letter from a well-known practicing psychiatrist, a devout Christian woman, who had this to say: "My own work consists in helping people to understand their unconscious sexual hindrances to personal relationships. Many of my fellow Christians seem to find this totally incompatible with 'Christianity.' Yet I am sure that psychological insights, fumbling though they still are, can ultimately only broaden and deepen true freedom of choice. And I suspect that today's young, sceptical as they are of traditional authority, are already making choices which, while uncomfortable to lovers of the *status quo*, are based on an attempt at personal morality more 'Christian' than that of many an 'obedient servant.' "

I quote this part of her letter, not only because I am in agreement with what she says, but also because it helps us to see that to understand "unconscious sexual hindrances to personal relationships," as she puts it, requires more than appeals to "traditional authority." This is why in this book I have sought to stress the controls which love itself exercises; and why I have sought also to urge that these "hindrances" so often are manifestations of failure in or distortion of love. Once we get love straight as the clue to the sexual existence upon which love itself is grounded, we can begin to work our way toward a "personal morality" which is essentially Christian both in approach and in content.

No appeal is required to divine fiat nor to laws laid down once for all in heaven. The implicit demands of love itself, deep in the human heart, can give guidance. Nor is this to deny the reality of what we call "sin." For sin is not violation of laws but breaking of love; and the path to a right vision of love is given to us when we contemplate love incarnate in Jesus Christ and in those who in his Spirit live and act in positive goodness and concern. The vision may be denied, in practice, but it remains in fact. The remarkable thing is that it speaks directly to the human heart, even the "sinful" human heart. In speaking to the heart, it shows up defects and distortions and enables us to grasp what can go wrong in our sexual existence as elsewhere in life.

The last chapter will return to this theme and attempt to sum up what we have been saying with special reference to the way in which such love is in accordance with the "grain of the universe." Here I wish to concentrate on one point—that an approach to sexual behavior such as we have urged is far from implying an easy and undemanding ethic. It is a commonplace in traditional Christian moral thinking that negative commands are easier to obey than positive ones. If I tell someone not to do this or that and he complies with what I have said, the matter is over and done with. On the other hand, if I give him a positive injunction—and if this injunction is also broad in its expectation—he will never fully live up to all the possibilities in view and he will certainly find it difficult to do even those which he undertakes. Now the imperative of love is like that. You can never love enough, since there will always be some areas in which that loving might have been expressed and was not, or where all possibilities of loving action were not carried out. This is why Whitehead once wrote that the teaching of Jesus, cast as it is in terms of great generality, provides both a goal toward which men can forever strive and a goal to urge them on in the striving. It leaves them unsatisfied because they know that "when they have done all that is commanded of them, they are still un-profitable servants," to cite a saying attributed to Jesus himself in the Gospels.

"In a communal religion," Whitehead wrote (he is here referring to primitive religions in which the person is submerged in social religious practices), "you study the will of God in order that he may preserve you; in a purified religion . . . you study his goodness in order to be like him."[4] These words appear in *Religion in the Making* where Whitehead is talking of the change from crude notions of deity as primarily power or coercive will, to those where, as in "the Galilean vision" found in the gospels, God is seen as persuasion, goodness, and love. Now morality comes under the same general rubric. In moral systems where people think in terms of absolute laws laid upon them from heaven and stop there, they are almost certain to look at moral imperatives as "pre-servative" in nature. But where they see morality as essentially concerned with an abiding but active good-ness or love, they will see its imperatives as guidance into the best ways of expressing that love. Under such a con-ception, everything is not "laid on the line." There will be loose ends, greater or less goods, variations in time and place and circumstance and hence in possibility of love's expression. And in our decisions we shall make mistakes and even cause unintentional hurt. But surely we should prefer this sort of world to one where (to con-

[4] Alfred North Whitehead, *Religion in the Making* (New York: Macmillan, 1926), p. 40. Used by permission.

tinue with some words of Whitehead) we are made to think of ourselves as "slavish subjects" of a "divine despot."[5] A Christian, at least, ought to be sufficiently taught by the gospel message here.

Thus our talk about love's controls is no invitation to complete laxity or to the abandonment of all standards. The controls are not exercised by force, to be sure; but failure to observe them can lead, and observably does lead, to less satisfying life in any ultimate sense and to less rewarding life in concrete experience here and now. As the father of "process" thought also saw, genuine morality "is always the aim at that union of harmony, intensity, and vividness"[6] which is possible for each person; and love in action is precisely harmonious, intense, and vivid. It is what we all want, at bottom; and the controls are present so that we may move toward the goal.

Unless this more open attitude is taken, we are continually in danger of assuming that the social conventions which *we* happen to approve are adequate to every age and in all situations. To think in that way, and to act upon it in imposing detailed rules, is the way of unthinking reactionary minds. "The result is that the world is shocked, or amused, by the sight of saintly old people hindering in the name of morality the removal

[5] Alfred North Whitehead, *Adventures of Ideas* (New York: Cambridge University Press, 1964), p. 289.
[6] Alfred North Whitehead, *Modes of Thought* (New York: Macmillan, 1938), p. 19.

of the obvious brutalities from a legal system'"[7]—so Whitehead wrote, to quote him once more. We have seen plenty of *that* in our own time, including opposition to laws giving justice to homosexuals, laws permitting contraception, laws on abortion, and much much else. But those who have accepted the argument we have presented here will be delivered in their thought about sexual contacts from such absurdity.

[7] Whitehead, *Adventures of Ideas*, p. 289.

THE RIGHT, BECAUSE LOVING, ORDERING OF SEXUAL LIFE 4

In the discussion of controls in sexual questions, the approach and the conclusions have, of course, been my own. I speak for nobody but myself, although I also speak *as* a Christian, a sexual being, and a supporter of "process" ideas. Nobody could say that all "process" theologians think alike; for example, we agree on certain assumptions and we have a common slant on things, but one of the characteristics of this conceptuality is its openness to diversity of interpretation. Certainly Christians too are agreed, by the nature of their faith, on important matters, but they differ on much else— and I know that my version of Christian faith is likely to be anathema to many who like me center their life and thought in Jesus Christ as God's signal disclosure in action for men. Even as a sexual being, my own experience and outlook are not presumed to be those of everybody (or anybody) else; they are my own, and necessarily so.

Yet at the same time, there is value in talking about these matters from one's own position as a man, a Christian, a thinker. Others may be helped thereby to think for themselves. It is possible that something has been said which will find a response in their own ways of understanding. I say all this because in this closing chapter I wish to discuss moral absolutes and relatives; to relate to these the controls considered in the preceding section; and finally to indicate the way in which, as it appears to me, a right because loving ordering of sexual life provides for us some genuine insight into how things really "go" in the world and how we men are meant to "go" in accordance with the cosmic "going." What I say is intended to be suggestive; it makes no pretense to being definitive.

When we talk about "absolutes," especially *moral* ones (as so many wish to do, especially if they feel troubled or threatened by the "permissiveness" of our time), we had better know what we mean. I presume that most of those who speak in this fashion are referring to some supposedly unalterable, eternal, established, and inescapable concepts and realities, be they moral or theological, to which men must adjust themselves because they are forever fixed in the very nature of things —or perhaps because they are taken to have been divinely revealed and divinely validated *as* absolute. And I presume that by "relatives" most people intend to indicate changeable and changing patterns of thought, whose significance is largely determined by their usefulness at a given time and place, by their sociological context, or by some other humanly available criteria. Their authority is not taken to be utterly binding, however important it may be here and now; they are caught up in an historical development which reflects the situation and circumstances of their appearance.

Now for the most part claims made about moral absolutes, and particularly for such absolutes in respect to sexual matters, rest back upon the prior belief that God is himself absolute, without relationships, with a moral demand whose detailed contents are fixed and final. Such a picture of God is taken to be a correct portrayal of the God of Western theism in its traditional form. He is all-powerful and he keeps everything, above all man, in utter subjection to himself. The American theologian-critic Nathan Scott has called such a deity "the God-thing"—and the term is appropriate, for only *things* seem never to change, always to be self-contained, open to no influence upon them. Of course, that is not really true even of "things," yet so it usually appears to us.

There is indeed a sense in which God *is* absolute, as I shall try to show in a minute and as I have already hinted in our first chapter. But Scott is surely correct in speaking of the general traditional picture of God as essentially "the conception of a supreme Being who, being eternally immutable and impassive, is forever unaffected by and consequently indifferent to all the endeavors and vicissitudes which make up the human story." For God so conceived, he adds, "man's earthly pilgrimage is, ultimately, of no account, since nothing that we do or fail to do can augment or detract from the static perfection that this God enjoys."[1]

Some may think that this description is only a bitter caricature of what traditonal theism has said. To a degree this is true, but the point is that this is the *impression* which many moderns have of that kind of theism and it is also the "working image" of God that has colored much piety and is back of much moralism. To show this we need only remark that while in principle such a God is not at all affected in himself by what "we do or fail to do," at the same time he is conceived to take an almost sadistic satisfaction in seeing that moral wrong, according to arbitrarily imposed standards, is punished up to the hilt. Nowhere is this seen more plainly than in what is said about his "attitude," as we might say, to sexual misbehavior. So much is this the case that in the ordinary man's mind sin is thought to be itself equated by God with "sex"!

God, I have said, *is* in a profound sense absolute—that is, he is the one enduring and abiding reality, not above and beyond all change but in and through all change. This I say as a Christian and a process theologian. And I must explain what I am getting at. God, then, is *absolutely* related to his creation. And the ancient so-called "metaphysical attributes of deity" are ways of saying that cosmic Love and the cosmic

[1] Nathan A. Scott, Jr., *The Wild Prayer of Longing* (New Haven: Yale University Press, 1971), p. 54.

Lover are everywhere at work (omnipresent), utterly wise (omniscient), the strongest agency in the world (omnipotent), persisting through all time (eternal), and beyond all creaturely understanding (infinite and im-measurable). So, in an abstract fashion we affirm that God *is*; but in a concrete way and as actually known and available, he is *as Love and Lover*, self-identified as such and unfailingly in relationship with the created world. His eternity is not timelessness but the fullest conceivable experience of time and history; and the association of that concept (eternity) with Greek ideas of impassibility and unchanging metaphysical identity are (for those who think in this process way) one of the tragic mistakes of Christian theology. Thus as he is known and as he concretely is, disclosing himself in action *for* what he is, he is no remote, abstract, and entirely absolute being. Rather, he is the One who *is* what he *does*, disclosing himself as caring for the world, suffering from or rejoicing in what happens in that world; and he cannot be conceived by us save as he has *some* creation (not necessarily or only this one that we know) in which and through which, for which and by which, he dynamically energizes in love.

I make bold to claim that this way of speaking about God is implicit in the biblical material and finds its culmination when a Man appears in whom the prior activity of God in caring is met by the response of the activity of man in loving surrender: namely, in Jesus Christ as the New Testament picture portrays him to us.

But it may well be asked, what on earth and sky has all this to do with the subject of the present book, with the human meaning of sexuality and with the implicit controls by love about which we have been speaking? I ask the reader to be a little patient; I hope that it will be demonstrated that what has just been said about God has enormous relevance to the matter under consideration. Before we get to the point, however, it will be convenient to say something more about what it is to be human, since what is said about man is usually indicative of what is thought about God, and vice versa.

We have seen that man is a psychosomatic (body-mind, stuff-spirit) complex, possessed of rationality and will; but what is even more important, that he is a creature who like all created entities has the quality of freedom—he may choose, within certain limits, of course, and he is so made that he can and does (or should) assume responsibility for the decisions which he makes. We have also insisted that man is a social being, related to and mutually dependent upon others of his kind. No man exists apart from that human belonging; we are all members one of another, knit together as the splendid Old Testament phrase tells us in "one bundle of life." Hence our developing personality, our personal becoming as men, and our sociality are two sides of the same thing: a dynamic movement toward the realization of potentiality, in association with and as participant in the total human situation or condition. Finally, we are made in or toward God's image; since God is Love, we are lovers-in-the-making. We tragically violate love, refusing to give ourselves in love, rejecting the love of others, hurting them in their capacity for love—this is our defection from our true human possibility as God intends it to be. So, we are sinners; but a Christian must add, redeemable sinners who in the event of Christ *have been* redeemed and who now are to accept and live in terms of the newness which in Christ has been effectually realized and visibly expressed in the historical process of human existence.

This is the basic view which both Christian thought and a process conceptuality make possible for us as the background of the human meaning of sexuality. And because human loving must be ordered or directed so that it will move in the right way, so also the sexuality which provides the physiological-psychological grounding for love must be ordered or directed in its expression in overt activity. I do not know whether I have succeeded here in making clear to the reader the intention of these last two or three pages. I hope so, for without such a grasp of the point that is being made, it is likely that he will once more assume that the word controls has been, and is being, used negatively. Far from it. What I want to show above all is that all this business of man's processive nature, his use of his potentialities, his free decisions, his responsibility, his sexual equipment and desires, and his human loving, hangs together and is *one* reality, *one* truth which we must accept and face. Only so can we understand ourselves and our relationship with others; only so can we begin to make sense of, find meaning in, and give value to our human sexuality.

It is obvious, of course, that most of us most of the time do not articulate this in words. We are too much occupied with the sheer business of living to do that.

But now and again we *do* think about ourselves and about who and what we are as men. The job of the theologian, the moralist, and the philosopher is to take our inchoate and vague feelings of human significance and seek to put them in some ordered way which will convey meaning to those who do him the honor of reading or hearing him. This is what I have been trying to do in the last few pages.

Very well . . . and what then? What is required is a return to the question of the ethics of sexual behavior; and here we must begin with the reassertion of the principle that the *only* moral absolute about which we can meaningfully speak is *love*. Love here includes God's own nature or character or essence and also the participated awareness of love which we know in our limited human way. The word is highly ambiguous, as we all know. Already we have had occasion to warn that it does not mean sentimentality, softness, cheap toleration of whatever happens. It is relationship in which there is giving and receiving, benevolence and good will, and yearning or desire for intimate union with others. In this inclusive yet somewhat austere sense, then, love is the one absolute; and it also includes within it righteousness or just dealing, outgoing goodness, concern for the welfare of other men, and so forth—all of which are ways in which love expresses itself. For our present interest, however, I emphasize that it includes the desire for and need of explicit sexual expression.

If love is the one absolute, it must also be said that in our human situation—finite, limited, influenced by the past of the race—the only way we can grasp that absolute is in a relative fashion. The absolute can be known and served only relatively. Some of the readers of this book may recall the saying of the Danish thinker Sören Kierkegaard, that we can be related to the absolute only in "relational ways." We do not have total, complete, final, and (as we might put it) absolute knowledge of the absolute which is love. We know it only in the specific situations in which we exist, with the demands that these make upon us, the opportunities they offer us, the barriers they erect to perfect comprehension, and the responsibilities which we have to take upon us where we are and as we are.

What this amounts to is that new occasions do indeed teach new duties—and as the poem by Lowell goes on to say, "time makes ancient good uncouth," or if not "uncouth," then irrelevant and inapplicable to *our* time. In and through the new occasions in the secular circumstances where we happen to be, God is evoking, enticing, soliciting, inviting, even requiring new kinds of response to his purpose of love-in-action in the world. This is why ancient codes, commandments, and the like have no absolute significance; they are the setting down of what our ancestors understood to be *their* duty and this (as we have seen) meant *their* particular way of responding to the divine imperative to live and act in love. They provide us with guidelines, if you will; but they are not once-and-for-all disclosures nor do they give us divine enactments handed down from heaven or somehow found imbedded in the human conscience. They are subject to revision and this revision is not a denial of them and the deep insight they contain, but a fulfilling, or effective bringing out (here we recall how Jesus claimed to "fulfill" the Torah, not to deny its validity for its own time), of what the older ways of thinking and stating the right standards of moral behavior were aiming at—sometimes better, sometimes worse, never exhaustively nor absolutely.

This approach is familiar enough for those who are aware of new movements in the field of moral theory. The "new breed" of thinkers on this subject are often condemned by their more conservative brethren, but in my judgment they have understood far better than the conservatives the central moral issues and the basically Christian way of looking at them. Thereby they have been brought to say something different about human responsibility in social relationships, the welfare state, and such questions as race, war, and the like, as well as about more personal matters like premarital sexual contacts, masturbation, divorce, contraception, abortion and medical ethics (transplants), and homosexuality. However much some of these views, and especially the ones having to do with sexual matters, may scandalize Christians brought up to believe that there is always a plain, straightforward, unchanging, and hence "absolute" set of moral requirements, the truth is that the newer attitude finds its validity in the gospel sayings about love, in the total impact of the figure of Jesus, in the Pauline epistles, and in the main thrust of the historical Christian moral tradition. That tradition has been tragically influenced, to be sure, by the anti-wordly, anti-sexual, docetic or gnostic ideas which got mixed up in early times with Christian thinking. Thus there has been a confusion of chastity with sexual negation, for example, rather than a recognition that chastity is "to will one thing," as Kierkegaard put it—or, in John Macmurray's words, it is "emotional sincerity." Nonetheless the Christian tradition has always held, in principle, to the centrality and absoluteness of love only; and Thomas Aquinas neatly captured this insight when he said, "The new law is Christ's love in men's hearts."

With all this in mind, we can now see why it is right to say that sexual behavior is ordered in its proper fashion when love is central to it and to all modes of sexual expression. This is not a repression or denial of man's freedom; it is, rather, a genuine fulfillment of such freedom. There is a lesser sort of so-called freedom which ought instead to be called license: doing whatever one wants when and as one wants it, regardless of consequences for oneself or others. But that is really not freedom at all. It is nothing but bondage to the impulses and instinctive responses of the moment, subject to change without notice and liable to produce a kind of existence which in the strictest sense of the word is dissipated—that is to say, scattered in all directions with no integrity and no point of reference. Against this not only Christians but secularistic humanists, too, would wish to protest. Both of them know that man is to act like a man and to be helped to become a man. There is nothing to be said for an entirely uncontrolled existence any more than there is any value in what Socrates spoke of as the unexamined life. Secular wisdom and Christian thought agree on this point; it is too bad that in many instances the lines of communication between them have been so poor that the agreement is unnoticed or forgotten. On the other hand, neither the Christian nor the humanist would deny the wonder and glory of sexual union, the enormous satisfaction that it can give, and the way in which two human beings feel at one in body and soul in their total selfhood when such union takes place under circumstances that are genuinely loving. There is nothing dirty, furtive, shameful, or in any sense wrong in the ecstacy of sexual contact; it can be wrong only when it is put in the context of selfishness, cruelty, impersonality, carelessness or irresponsibility, or when it is made into the be-all and end-all of human existence and therefore is inordinate or disproportionate.

W. A. Beardslee has written a fine book on Christian hope as seen from the perspective of process thought.[2] He begins his discussion with a chapter on the sexual basis for hope. In doing this he divides sexuality into two aspects, one of them the physical union of two bodies, the other the procreation and care of children. It is in the latter only that he seems able to find a paradigm for hope, since it is there that a man and woman are enabled to see the future for which they hope, working itself out in their offspring. I believe that Beardslee is correct in what he affirms and wrong in what he appears to deny. I do not think that actual sexual union is a seeking for some indefinite infinity, or longing for totality, as he puts it. On the contrary, it is seeking for,

[2] W. A. Beardslee, *A House for Hope* (Philadelphia: Westminster Press, 1972).

and finding in the present reality of total sharing of body and spirit, an experience which itself is the promise of the future. My reason for saying this is very simple. Love has about it the quality of everlastingness; and as Beardslee himself recognizes it can be put like this, "When I say 'I love you,' I am also saying *sotto voce* 'for ever.'" Of such love sexual union is the chief mode of expression, humanly speaking. Hence in that union, there *is* an implicit hope.

In his book Beardslee remarks how in much music and song sexual union and death are brought together. The *Liebestod* in Wagner's *Tristan und Isolde* would be a case in point; so would the use by some writers of the phrase "the little death" to describe the moment of orgasm in sexual union. But I believe that this association can be misinterpreted. As I see it, it does not mean at the *deepest* level the loss of identity on the part of either of the partners, although some have taken it to suggest just that. Rather, I see here a strange witness to the fact that in the ecstatic union of bodies there is a loss of *self-for-self's-sake,* but a finding of *self-for-the-other's sake.* That is the agony which accompanies the ecstacy; it is the pain which comes when self, in one sense, is given up so that self in *another* sense may be discovered.

And that loss and gain is a focal disclosure of what must be true of all living which is in accordance with the way the world goes underneath superficial appearances and the obvious details we usually notice. Life is in giving and in receiving—in mutual relationships, as I have so often put this fact—and in such giving as well as in such receiving, there is bound to be suffering, "the sweet sorrow of love" of which a rather sentimental popular song once spoke.

Thus we come back at the end of our discussion to the necessity for seeing human sexuality as the ground of human love. In that context we can also recognize *why* such controls as have been suggested are for a positive purpose—to secure the reality and wonder, the glory and ecstacy, of love in all its richness. We ought never be afraid to love; we ought never be afraid to receive love; we ought never be afraid to live and act in love. This is as near to being absolute as anything in human experience. At the very same time and by the same token, we ought always to be prepared so to act in love that love itself will be the master motif, giving significance to the pleasure and gratification which sexual contacts provide.

Basic to it all is the truth stated in a wonderful sentence found in the ancient Maundy Thursday Liturgy of the Western Church: *ubi caritas et amor, Deus ibi est* ("where self-giving and love are to be found, there God is also to be found"). Tolstoy once said the same thing, "Where love is, there God is." The controls of which I have spoken have as their sole purpose the securing of that glorious truth.